Contents

PERSPECTIVE
OF
CONSCIOUSNESS

Beyond Appearances, Beneath Beliefs

Sunil Subbramaniyam

तत्त्वमसि – Thou art that

A reminder of the essence within us all

INDIA · SINGAPORE · MALAYSIA

ISBN
Paperback 979-8-89777-923-9
Hardcase 979-8-89961-880-2

Preface

This book began as a whisper—an inner urge to explore the nature of reality, question what lies beneath what we see, and gather the threads of perspective that so often go unnoticed. Over time, that whisper grew into a voice and eventually into the collection of stories, reflections, and questions that now rest in your hands.

I am eternally grateful to some remarkable souls who have brought this vision to life. In 2024, I had the privilege of attending a retreat in Goa led by my mentor and teacher in hypnotherapy, Nivedita Awasthi Sharma. It was there that I met a group of kindred spirits—Nishant, Resham, Ashish, Himali, Jayshree, Shilpi, Shireen, and Anahita—who not only held space for my thoughts but also held me accountable to complete this book. Their encouragement was a quiet yet constant reminder that what I had to say mattered.

To Ribu and Tejo, my dearest friends and unwavering support pillars—you have seen me through doubts and drafts, and your belief in me has been the foundation I've dared to build. Thank you for walking this journey beside me.

And finally, to my son, Angad Subbramaniyam, whose small yet profound thoughts and one-liners often leave me marvelling at the depth of his wisdom. You remind me daily that insight doesn't always come from years—it sometimes comes from innocence.

This book is not a guide or a conclusion. It is an invitation to pause, to ponder, to peel back the layers of what we call real and to discover the truths that reside beyond appearances and beneath beliefs. I hope these pages serve as gentle mirrors, helping you see the world—and yourself—a little differently.

With humility and hope,

Sunil Subbramaniyam

Chapter 1

The Power of Perspectives

A Lesson in Perspectives

I've always been intrigued by the concept of perspectives. I've thought about it deeply, often questioning what it truly means and how it shapes our lives. I struggled to define and grasp the depth of its power for years. The breakthrough came during a conversation with two remarkable individuals who helped me uncover the true essence of perspectives. One of them was my mentor, whom I had the privilege of working with during the early stages of my career in an IT organisation.

It happened during a particularly challenging period. I was overwhelmed, grappling with a complex situation that seemed to have no clear solution. My mind was racing, my thoughts tangled with anxiety and uncertainty. My mentor noticed my distress and approached me.

"What's troubling you?" he asked gently.

After I explained the situation in detail, he said something unexpected: "Come, let's go for a walk."

I wasn't in the mood for a walk, but I reluctantly agreed. As we walked in silence for a few moments, he asked me a simple yet puzzling question:

"Do you know what a conversation really means?"

Confused and irritated, I replied, "Yes, of course. It's what we're having right now."

He smiled knowingly and asked another question. "How many types of conversations do you think there are?"

My irritation began to grow. "Professor, is this leading to any advice about my problem?"

He nodded attentively and indicated that I should respond. I listed my thoughts: "Formal conversations, informal interactions, casual dialogues. Additionally, I have experience with feedback discussions from a human resources perspective."

He interrupted, smiling. "Theoretically correct, but let me share something that might shift your perspective, especially regarding your current dilemma. In any situation, there are really just two kinds of conversations."

His words piqued my curiosity despite my earlier frustration. "I'm listening," I said, eager for clarity.

He explained:

Sunil, there are two fundamental types of conversations:

First-Order Conversations

These are conversations that cannot be questioned or contested. They represent facts. For instance, your name is Sunil, and that's a first-order conversation. You're also sitting on a chair—that is a fact. Similarly, the situation you're facing exists as a fact. It's something you cannot deny or change.

Second-Order Conversations

These are the stories, interpretations, and narratives we create about the facts. For example, four people might describe you, Sunil, differently based on their interactions with you. Similarly, the way you've interpreted your situation—your feelings of anxiety and the overwhelming narrative you've constructed—is a second-order conversation.

Here's the key: while you cannot alter a first-order conversation, you have complete control over the second-order conversations. You can step back, detach from your personal point of view, and examine the situation from different angles. Often, resolving a problem isn't about changing the fact itself—it's about identifying which second-order conversation needs to be addressed to shift your perspective and find a solution."

His words struck a chord deep within me. I stood there, processing this profound insight. Suddenly, it all made sense. My anxiety was not rooted in the situation itself, but in the story, I had created around it. By reframing the narrative and considering the perspectives of others involved, I could see the situation with greater clarity. With this newfound approach, I resolved the issue more quickly than I had thought possible.

Reflection on the Lesson

That day, my mentor taught me one of the most powerful lessons on perspectives. Often, it's not the situation that holds us back but the narratives we construct around it. By identifying and reshaping these narratives, we can unlock new ways of thinking and acting. This simple yet profound understanding of first-order and second-order conversations has stayed with me ever since, guiding me through countless challenges in my personal and professional life.

As we continue this journey through the book, we'll explore how shifting perspectives can transform not only how we see the world but also how we live within it.

In life, we all experience the world through our unique lenses, which are shaped by our backgrounds, experiences, values, and beliefs. Our perspectives influence how we perceive situations, respond to challenges, and make decisions. Understanding and mastering the power of perspectives can transform how we navigate our personal and professional lives and, in turn, lead to greater fulfilment, growth, and success.

The Role of Perspectives in Shaping Our Reality

In life, we often find ourselves in situations where our perspectives differ from those of others. We may face conflicts with colleagues, misunderstandings with loved ones, or struggles with personal growth, all of which stem from how we see the world.

For instance, two people can experience the same event but interpret it differently. One person might see a setback as a failure, while another might view it as an opportunity for growth. One person might feel frustrated by a challenging situation, while another might embrace it as a learning experience.

Our perspectives dictate how we interpret events, handle stress, and engage with the world around us. They are not fixed or permanent; rather, they can be changed, expanded, and enriched.

The Importance of Expanding Your Perspectives

One of the most powerful things we can do for ourselves is to actively work on expanding our perspectives. When we challenge ourselves to view the world through different lenses, we open ourselves to new ideas, experiences, and possibilities.

Imagine being able to see every challenge as an opportunity, embrace uncertainty with curiosity, and face adversity with resilience. This is the power of perspective—the ability to shift how we interpret the world around us. This, in turn, will lead to a shift in how we interpret ourselves in the world around us. This can be supremely life-changing.

Expanding our perspectives doesn't mean abandoning our beliefs or values. Instead, it means being open to considering alternative viewpoints, listening actively to others, and recognising that our way of seeing things is just one way among many. By embracing a broader perspective, we can become more adaptable, empathetic, and empowered personally and professionally.

How to Shift Your Perspective

Shifting your perspective doesn't require drastic changes in your life. It's about developing the ability to step back and see things from different angles. Here are a few practical steps you can take to begin shifting your perspective:

Practice Empathy – When encountering someone with a different opinion or experience, try to understand their origin. Ask questions, listen without judgement, and be open to learning from their perspective.

Challenge Your Assumptions – We all have biases and assumptions that influence how we see the world. Take time to examine your assumptions and consider how they might shape your perspective.

Seek New Experiences – Travelling, meeting new people, or trying new activities can expose you to different ways of thinking and living. These experiences can help you broaden your perspective and challenge your worldview.

Practice Mindfulness – By staying present and observing your thoughts without judgement, you can understand how your current perspective influences your emotions and reactions.

Embrace Change – Change is inevitable, and it often brings with it new perspectives. Rather than resisting change, embrace it as an opportunity for growth and transformation.

Key Understandings of Perspectives

As we conclude this chapter, here are some key takeaways about the concept of perspectives:

Our Experiences shape our Perspectives – Our past experiences, beliefs, and values influence our worldview. This means that two people can experience the same event but interpret it differently.

Our Perspectives Are Not Fixed – Perspectives are not permanent. They can be expanded, challenged, and changed as we grow and learn.

Our Perspective Shapes Our Reality – How we see the world directly impacts how we experience it. Our perspectives influence our emotions, actions, and outcomes in life.

Shifting Perspectives Leads to Growth – We open ourselves to new possibilities, greater empathy, and personal growth by embracing new perspectives.

We Have the Power to Choose Our Perspective – Ultimately, we can choose how we view the world. We can see challenges as opportunities, setbacks as lessons, and adversity as a path to growth.

The power of perspective lies in its ability to shape how we experience and respond to the world. As we progress in this book, we will explore ways to harness this power to create lasting change in our lives.

Chapter 2

Perspectives of Success

Success is a word that captivates us, driving our determination. It's a term etched into the fabric of our aspirations, whether it's excelling in our careers, building meaningful relationships, or accomplishing personal milestones. Yet, beneath its shiny exterior lies a profound truth: success is anything but straightforward.

What makes one person's triumph feel hollow and another's fulfilment so radiant? The answer lies in *perspective*. Success is not a one-size-fits-all concept; it is a deeply personal experience shaped by our unique backgrounds, values, and life stories. For one person, it might be the corner office and financial security. For another, it might be the joy of nurturing a family or making a difference in the community.

Imagine success as a kaleidoscope—each turn offers a new view, revealing patterns as distinct as the individuals seeking it. This chapter will take you through these shifting patterns, exploring the multifaceted nature of success through four distinct lenses: the material, emotional, social, and holistic perspectives.

But this is more than a theoretical discussion. Through a compelling story of two individuals with starkly different ideas of success, you'll see how perspective shapes what we strive for and how we experience life's victories.

As we embark on this journey, ask yourself: What does success mean to me? The answer may surprise, challenge, or even inspire you to redefine your path entirely. Let's explore the many shades of success together.

A Story of Success

Let me begin with a story about Ramesh, a software engineer, and his neighbour, Kavita, a homemaker.

Ramesh had always been driven by ambition. From a young age, he was taught that success was measured by tangible achievements—high-paying jobs, big promotions, and impressive titles. His dream was clear: to earn a high salary, climb the corporate ladder, and retire early. Every day, he woke up early, sat in traffic, and spent long hours in front of his computer screen at the office. Weekends weren't a break for him; they were filled with networking events, industry seminars, and pursuing additional professional certifications. Ramesh prided himself on his ability to work tirelessly, always thinking about the next step, the next promotion, the next raise. On the surface, Ramesh seemed to embody success—he owned a luxurious car, lived in a well-furnished apartment in the city, had a sizeable bank account, and was respected by his peers for his work ethic and accomplishments.

In contrast, Kavita lived a quieter life. She was a homemaker and a mother, and her days were filled with caring for her family and managing her household. From early morning preparing breakfast to afternoons running errands for the family, she found purpose in the small, everyday tasks. Kavita was not interested in high-profile careers or extravagant possessions. Still, instead, she found immense joy in simple pleasures—baking for her neighbours, sharing stories with her children, and volunteering at the local library. She didn't have a title like "manager" or "director," but to her, every small act of kindness she offered was a measure of success. She found peace in knowing that she was present for her family, and her contentment came from the emotional connections she nurtured, not from accumulating wealth or status.

One evening, during a power outage in their neighbourhood, Ramesh and Kavita happened to be having a conversation while sitting outside their homes. The sky was unusually clear, and the gentle breeze seemed to add a layer of calm to the stillness around them.

"Kavita," Ramesh said, gazing into the night, "Don't you ever feel like you're missing out? Wouldn't you like to do something bigger with your life? Maybe work on a grand project, travel the world, or build an empire?" He paused, glancing at his watch. "You know, I've always been told that success is about climbing higher, achieving more, and having more. But I don't see you chasing any of that. Don't you feel like you're... settling?"

Kavita looked at him thoughtfully. A smile tugged at the corner of her lips as she replied, Bigger? What could be bigger than shaping my children's lives or making a difference in my community? My success isn't measured by money or titles, but by the love, connection, and peace I experience daily. You see, Ramesh, my days may not be filled with grand meetings or big decisions, but I find fulfilment in the small moments— the laughter around the dinner table, the joy I see when I help someone in need, the knowledge that I'm creating a space of love for my family to grow and thrive.

Ramesh blinked, taken aback. Her words hit him in a way he hadn't expected. He had always equated success with outward accomplishments—expensive possessions, promotions, and accolades. But here was Kavita, a woman with little concern for societal standards, living what appeared to be a deeply fulfilling life grounded in simple values. She didn't need recognition to feel valued. She wasn't chasing after any external markers of success. She was content with her life and role, which was the most powerful thing she seemed to possess.

Ramesh couldn't help but think about his own life. He had spent years working for promotions and higher pay, striving to impress his colleagues and pushing himself harder and harder to pursue external validation. Yet, despite all his achievements, something was missing. He couldn't remember the last time he had felt truly content. His work was stressful, his relationships were strained, and he rarely had time for what truly brought him joy. Was his success, as defined by society, really making him happy? Or had he been blindly chasing an ideal that wasn't his own?

The conversation with Kavita stayed with Ramesh for days. He couldn't stop reflecting on her words. What if success wasn't about climbing the corporate ladder, acquiring more material things, or impressing others? What if true success was about finding contentment in the present moment, appreciating the little things, and nurturing the emotional bonds that truly mattered?

As time passed, Ramesh began to slowly change his perspective. He started by re-evaluating his values. He realised he had been chasing a version of success largely dictated by external expectations—society, his colleagues, and even his family's unspoken ideals. But he began to ask himself: What do I truly value? What kind of life do I want to create for myself?

Ramesh started to embrace the idea that success didn't have to mean more money or a higher title. Instead, it could mean pursuing work aligned with his passions, spending more time with loved ones, and investing in his emotional and mental well-being. He began to set boundaries with work, prioritising his personal life and making time for hobbies he had long neglected, such as photography and gardening.

He also started volunteering at a local shelter, something he had always wanted to do but had never made time for. As he gave back to the community, he felt a sense of fulfilment he had never experienced in his corporate career. The joy he found in these simple acts made him realise that success was not just about climbing higher but also about growing deeper—deeper into self-awareness, personal relationships, and understanding the world around him.

Ramesh's journey wasn't an overnight transformation. It took time for him to let go of his old definition of success and even more time to embrace his new way of thinking fully. But he found his life richer and more meaningful over the following months. The stress of work was still there, but it no longer defined him. His self-worth was no longer tied to his job title or his pay check. Instead, he found fulfilment in the love and peace he shared with his family, the impact he made through small acts of kindness and the time he spent nurturing his passions.

Ramesh learned from Kavita that success wasn't external—it was deeply internal. It wasn't about what others thought of you or how much you had. It was about living in alignment with your values, creating meaningful relationships, and finding joy in the present moment.

Let's delve into four different perspectives of success, each offering valuable insights into approaching this multifaceted concept.

The Material Perspective

Success is synonymous with wealth, possessions, and social status for many. This perspective is often shaped by societal norms that equate financial prosperity with achievement.

While there's no denying the importance of financial stability, the material perspective can sometimes lead to a hollow pursuit. Accumulating wealth for its own sake, without aligning it with personal values or purpose, often results in dissatisfaction. However, when material success is seen as a means to achieve broader goals—such as providing for one's family or creating opportunities for others—it takes on a more meaningful dimension.

The Emotional Perspective

Emotional success centres on inner peace, happiness, and fulfilment. It's about waking up each day with purpose and going to bed with a sense of contentment.

This perspective prioritises relationships, personal growth, and emotional well-being over external achievements. Someone with this viewpoint may succeed in maintaining a healthy work-life balance, fostering meaningful connections, or pursuing passions that bring them joy.

Learning to navigate societal expectations is a challenge for those who adopt this perspective. They may face criticism for not pursuing traditional markers of success, but their resilience and self-awareness often enable them to stay true to their path.

The Social Perspective

From the social perspective, success is about the impact one makes on others. It's not just about personal achievements but about contributing to the greater good.

People with this viewpoint find fulfilment in acts of service, community involvement, and mentorship. Their success is measured by the positive changes they bring to the lives of others.

Take, for example, a teacher who dedicates their life to educating underprivileged children. Their salary may not reflect societal standards of success, but the lives they transform tell a different story. Success is about legacy for them—leaving the world a better place than they found it.

The Holistic Perspective

The holistic perspective combines elements of material, emotional, and social success. It recognises that true success is multidimensional and requires balance and alignment across different aspects of life.

A person with a holistic view doesn't see career advancement and personal well-being as mutually exclusive. They strive for harmony, understanding that success in one area should not come at the expense of another. For example, a successful entrepreneur might prioritise business growth and spending quality time with their family, ensuring that their achievements contribute to their happiness and fulfilment.

Key Understandings of the Concept

Success Is Personal – There is no universal definition of success. It's a deeply individual concept shaped by your values, experiences, and aspirations.

Success Evolves – What you consider successful today may change as you grow and your priorities shift. Be open to redefining success at different stages of life.

Balance Is Key – True success often involves finding harmony among material, emotional, social, and holistic dimensions. Neglecting one for the sake of another can lead to imbalance and dissatisfaction.

Perspective Shapes Reality – How you view success determines your path. Reflect on your beliefs and ensure they align with your authentic self rather than societal expectations.

As you reflect on this chapter, consider which perspective of success resonates most with you. Are you chasing material wealth, seeking emotional fulfilment, striving for social impact, or pursuing a balance of all three? Remember, success is not a destination but a journey; your perspective will guide the way.

Chapter 3

Perspectives of Failure

Failure!!! The word itself is enough to trigger discomfort, regret, and even fear. For most of us, failure is something to avoid at all costs, a mark of inadequacy or incompetence. But what if we told you that failure is not the villain we've made it out to be? What if, instead, it's a misunderstood ally—one that teaches, shapes, and propels us towards growth?

It's something most people strive to avoid at all costs. Yet, if you look closely, failure is also a teacher, a motivator, and a stepping stone. Just like success, failure isn't one-dimensional. Its meaning, impact, and value depend entirely on the perspective through which we view it.

Failure, much like success, is a multifaceted concept. Its impact depends entirely on how we perceive it. For some, failure is the end of the road; for others, it's the first step on a new path. This chapter will explore failure from four perspectives: personal, professional, societal, and growth-oriented. Through real-life stories and reflections, we'll uncover how embracing failure can transform our lives.

In this chapter, we will unravel the concept of failure through four distinct perspectives: the personal, professional, societal, and growth-oriented views. By understanding these angles, you'll learn to embrace failure as an integral part of growth rather than a roadblock to your aspirations.

The Story of Ravi and the Unexpected Lesson

Ravi was a young entrepreneur with an ambitious vision. Armed with a business degree and a fiery passion, he launched his first startup, confident it would revolutionise the e-commerce industry. Six months later, reality struck. His business was in shambles, with dwindling funds and no sustainable plan. Ravi's dream had collapsed, and with it, his confidence.

Feeling defeated, Ravi confided in his mentor, Anika. "I've failed," he admitted, his voice heavy with despair. "Maybe I'm not cut out for this."

Anika responded simply: "What if failure isn't the opposite of success but a part of it?"

She explained that failure often serves as a mirror, reflecting areas that need improvement. "Success stories are rarely linear, Ravi. They're full of setbacks, missteps, and lessons. Your failure isn't a verdict—it's feedback."

Taking her advice, Ravi spent the next two years rebuilding himself. He studied his mistakes, refined his strategy, and launched a second venture. This time, he succeeded beyond his wildest dreams.

Let's explore four distinct perspectives on failure, each providing valuable insights into how we can navigate and embrace this multifaceted concept.

The Personal Perspective of Failure

On a personal level, failure can feel like an attack on our self-worth. A failed relationship, a missed goal, or an unfulfilled promise can lead us to question our abilities and identity. Many equate failure with inadequacy, internalising it as a permanent flaw rather than a temporary setback.

However, failure is only as powerful as the meaning we assign to it. Consider this reframe: failure is an event, not an identity. When we view failure as a moment in time rather than a defining characteristic, we liberate ourselves from its grip.

Take Thomas Edison, for example. When asked about his 10,000 failed attempts to invent the light bulb, he famously replied, "I have not failed. I've just found 10,000 ways that won't work." This mindset—seeing failure as a stepping stone rather than a dead end—is key to personal resilience.

The Professional Perspective of Failure

In the workplace, failure can feel catastrophic. A botched project, a missed promotion, or a failed venture often leaves us questioning our professional competence. However, failure is increasingly recognised as a valuable asset in the corporate world.

Consider the concept of "failing fast" in tech startups. Companies like Google and Amazon encourage experimentation, knowing failure is often the precursor to innovation. By treating failure as a learning opportunity, professionals can develop new skills, refine their strategies, and ultimately achieve greater success.

One powerful example is the story of J.K. Rowling. Before she became one of the most successful authors of all time, Rowling faced numerous rejections from publishers. Had she given up, the world would never have known the magic of Harry Potter. Her journey highlights how professional setbacks can be stepping stones to incredible achievements.

The Societal Perspective of Failure

Society has a complicated relationship with failure. On one hand, it idolises success stories; on the other, it stigmatises failure. This societal pressure can make failure feel even more daunting, as the fear of judgement often amplifies our sense of shame.

However, the most celebrated figures in history often failed repeatedly before succeeding. Albert Einstein, for instance, was considered a poor student and was even expelled from school. Walt Disney was fired from a newspaper for "lacking creativity." These stories remind us that societal perceptions of failure are often shortsighted.

By challenging societal norms, we can redefine failure as a badge of courage—a testament to our willingness to take risks and grow. Imagine a world where failure is celebrated as much as success, where lessons learned are valued as highly as achievements.

The Growth-Oriented Perspective of Failure

The most transformative way to view failure is through a growth-oriented lens. This perspective sees failure not as an obstacle but as a catalyst for personal development.

Failure teaches us resilience, adaptability, and self-awareness. It forces us to confront our limitations and encourages us to push beyond them. Through failure, we learn to pivot, innovate, and persevere.

Consider the story of Steve Jobs. After being ousted from Apple, the company he co-founded, Jobs could have retreated into obscurity. Instead, he used the experience to grow, founding Pixar and eventually returning to Apple to lead it into an era of unprecedented success.

From a growth-oriented perspective, failure is not inevitable but essential. It's the fertile ground from which innovation, creativity, and breakthroughs emerge.

Key Understandings of the Concept

Failure Is Feedback – Failure, at its core, is one of life's most honest teachers. Each setback provides us with invaluable insights into what went wrong, what could be improved, and where we might focus our efforts next. It's easy to view failure as a negative experience, but when reframed, it becomes a diagnostic tool. Think of failure as the world's saying, "Here's where you can grow."

Take a failed project at work, for instance. Instead of labelling it a disaster, ask yourself: Did I misunderstand the requirements? Could I have communicated more effectively? Was my planning thorough enough? Each question leads to actionable insights, turning what once felt like a dead end into a roadmap for progress.

When we embrace failure as feedback, we transform it into a constructive force. We move from self-criticism to self-improvement, recognising that failure isn't the enemy—it's the process of refinement.

Failure Builds Resilience – Facing failure repeatedly can feel disheartening, but it strengthens our ability to bounce back over time. Resilience is like a muscle: the more it's exercised, the stronger it becomes. Every time we encounter failure and persevere, we build our capacity to handle adversity.

Consider athletes who lose crucial games or performers who face public rejection. Each loss, though painful, teaches them to recover, recalibrate, and continue striving. They learn to separate temporary setbacks from permanent defeats.

This resilience extends beyond our professional lives. It helps us cope with personal struggles, overcome disappointments, and maintain our mental well-being. Over time, we begin to see failure not as a final judgement but as a temporary hurdle—one we're fully equipped to overcome.

Failure Is Universal – No matter how successful someone appears, failure is a universal experience. Even the most accomplished individuals—world leaders, innovators, artists, and entrepreneurs—have faced moments of failure. Understanding this universality helps us to feel less isolated when we stumble.

Acknowledging that failure is a shared human experience fosters self-compassion. It reminds us that failing doesn't mean we're unworthy or incapable—it simply means we're human.

This perspective also helps us reframe how we perceive others' success. When we see someone thriving, we often overlook the struggles that preceded their achievements. By recognising that failure is an integral part of every success story, we can appreciate our journey with greater patience and empathy.

Failure Fuels Growth – Failure has a transformative power when viewed through a growth-oriented lens. It pushes us to confront our limitations, rethink our strategies, and adapt in ways we might never have considered otherwise. Growth often demands discomfort, and failure provides the necessary friction to spark change.

Take the story of a business that collapses due to poor financial planning. While the immediate outcome may feel devastating, it forces the entrepreneur to develop better budgeting skills, refine their business model, and approach their next venture with greater wisdom.

Growth isn't just about overcoming failure; it's about leveraging it. When we view failure as an opportunity to learn, it shifts from a roadblock to a stepping stone. It fuels our creativity, sharpens our focus, and prepares us for greater challenges ahead.

Embracing These Truths

When we internalise these key understandings, failure begins to lose its sting. Instead of fearing it, we learn to welcome it as a natural and necessary part of the journey. We gain clarity, strength, and insight with each failure, moving closer to the success we seek. Failure isn't just a momentary setback—it's an essential ingredient in growth and fulfilment.

When viewed with the right perspective, failure is a gift—a stepping stone to a better, more enlightened version of yourself. As we continue this journey, let's delve deeper into how failure shapes resilience and how you can harness its power to propel yourself toward success.

Are you ready to see failure in a new light? Let's turn the page and begin.

Chapter 4

Perspectives of Abundance

Imagine waking up each day feeling a sense of possibility, believing that life offers more than enough for you to thrive. Abundance is not just about having material wealth or achieving success; it's about how we see and experience the world. It's about recognising the opportunities, connections, and beauty surrounding us, even in the most challenging circumstances.

While scarcity whispers fear, convincing us that there's never enough time, money, success, or love, abundance shouts possibility. It's the belief that life is generous, that challenges can be met with creativity, and that sharing enriches rather than diminishes. It's a mindset shift from "I can't" to "How can I?" and from "What if I lose?" to "What can I give?"

Abundance isn't about turning a blind eye to reality or denying challenges. It's about redefining those challenges as stepping stones, understanding that every problem carries the seed of opportunity. It's about gratitude—seeing the good in what you already have and letting that gratitude pave the way for more. It's about collaboration—realising that lifting others doesn't lower you but strengthens everyone involved.

This chapter will delve into what abundance truly means, beyond surface-level notions of wealth and success. Through stories, perspectives, and practical insights, we'll uncover how adopting an abundance mindset can transform how we think, live, and interact with the world. By the end of this journey, you'll see abundance not as a distant ideal but as a way of life within your grasp, waiting to be embraced.

The Tale of the Two Farmers

In a drought-prone village nestled between rolling hills and arid plains, two farmers, Raj and Aman, lived side by side. The village had been experiencing declining rainfall for years, leaving its inhabitants struggling to grow enough food to sustain their families. Raj and Aman, like all the villagers, relied on their small plots of land for survival.

Raj, a seasoned farmer, often sat under a tree, gazing at his dry fields and cursing his luck. "The skies have betrayed us," he would mutter to himself. As the seasons passed, his frustration grew. When it was time to sow seeds, Raj hesitated, planting only half of his usual crop. "Why waste seeds when there isn't enough water to nurture them?" he reasoned. Raj's days were filled with worry, and his mind was consumed with fear of failure. His stress took a toll on his health and relationships, further deepening his sense of scarcity.

On the other hand, Aman viewed the situation with a different lens. While he acknowledged the harsh reality of the drought, he refused to be defeated by it. "Nature always finds a way to heal," he would tell himself. Aman decided to adapt. He spent days digging trenches around his fields to capture and store every drop of rainwater. He sought information about drought-resistant crops and experimented with planting techniques requiring less water.

But Aman didn't stop there. He believed that abundance multiplied when shared. He gathered the villagers, sharing his techniques and giving away some of his drought-resistant seeds.

"If we work together, we can make the best of what we have," he encouraged.

Months passed, and the results were striking. Raj's fields yielded a meagre harvest, just enough to scrape by. Aman's fields, however, flourished. The trenches he dug had captured enough water to sustain his crops and his choice of drought-resistant plants paid off. Moreover, Aman's willingness to share his knowledge inspired other villagers, creating a ripple effect of innovation and hope.

When Raj saw Aman's thriving farm, he approached him in frustration. "How is it that you succeeded while the rest of us barely survived?" he asked. Aman smiled and said, "It's not just about the rain or the land. It's about how you choose to see the situation. While you focused on what you didn't have, I focused on what I could do with what I had."

This story of Raj and Aman teaches us a profound truth: abundance isn't about the external resources we possess; it's about the internal mindset we cultivate. Aman's perspective of abundance allowed him to see opportunities where others saw limitations, foster creativity and resilience, and multiply his success through collaboration and generosity.

We all face droughts—moments of scarcity, challenges, and setbacks. How we respond defines the harvest we reap. By embracing a mindset of abundance, we unlock the potential to thrive, not just survive, even in the toughest of times. Let's delve into some of the perspectives in this mindset:

The Perspective of Gratitude

Gratitude is the foundation of abundance. When we focus on what we have rather than what we lack, our mindset shifts from scarcity to sufficiency. Gratitude trains our brain to recognise the positive aspects of life, making us more optimistic and open to opportunities.

Imagine waking up each day and listing three things you're grateful for. It could be as simple as a warm cup of coffee, the support of loved ones, or the ability to pursue your goals. By doing this, you enhance your mood and reinforce the belief that life is full of gifts waiting to be appreciated.

Gratitude creates a ripple effect. When you're grateful, you're more likely to share your positivity with others, fostering stronger relationships and a greater sense of connection.

The Perspective of Opportunity

An abundance mindset sees challenges as opportunities for growth. Whereas a scarcity perspective focuses on obstacles, abundance encourages us to look beyond the problem and find creative solutions.

Consider a struggling business owner who, instead of dwelling on declining sales, uses the downturn as an opportunity to innovate. By identifying untapped markets or introducing new services, they survive and thrive.

This perspective requires flexibility and resilience. It teaches us to view setbacks as stepping stones, reminding us that every situation holds the potential for growth and learning, no matter how difficult.

The Perspective of Generosity

Abundance thrives on giving. When we give—whether it's time, knowledge, or resources—we create a cycle of abundance that benefits everyone involved. Generosity fosters goodwill, trust, and collaboration, all contributing to a more abundant life.

Take Aman from the earlier story. His willingness to share his farming techniques didn't diminish his success; it amplified it. Generosity works the same way in our lives. By helping others succeed, we build support networks that enrich us as well.

This perspective challenges the scarcity-driven belief that giving diminishes our resources. Instead, it shows that generosity multiplies abundance, creating more opportunities for everyone.

The Perspective of Possibility

The perspective of possibility is about envisioning a world without limitations. It's about dreaming big and believing that we can achieve greatness. When we adopt this perspective, we free ourselves from the constraints of fear and self-doubt, opening the door to new opportunities.

Take innovators like Elon Musk or Oprah Winfrey. Their lives exemplify the power of possibility. They didn't let societal norms or personal challenges limit their vision. Instead, they imagined a better future and took steps to make it a reality.

Possibility fuels ambition and creativity. It encourages us to think beyond our current circumstances and strive for something greater.

Key Understandings of the Concept

Abundance Starts with Gratitude – Gratitude is the foundation of an abundant mindset. When we focus on what we already have—relationships, opportunities, or simple joys—we shift our perspective from scarcity to fulfilment. Instead of dwelling on what's missing, we recognise and celebrate the good in our lives. Gratitude fosters positivity, creating a mental space where possibilities thrive. It's not about settling for less but appreciating the stepping stones that can lead to greater things.

When you start each day with a grateful heart, you prime yourself to notice opportunities and blessings, opening the door to abundance in all areas of life.

Abundance Encourages Resilience – An abundant mindset transforms challenges into opportunities for growth. Life will inevitably throw obstacles our way, but how we perceive them determines our ability to overcome them. With abundance, setbacks become lessons, and failures become feedback. Instead of seeing a closed door, we start looking for a window—or even create one ourselves. This resilience fuels innovation, adaptability, and confidence, empowering us to face uncertainty with courage. It's not about avoiding challenges but about approaching them with the belief that solutions exist and that each step forward adds to our strength and wisdom.

Abundance Is Amplified by Generosity – One of the most profound truths about abundance is that it grows when shared. Generosity—whether it's giving time, knowledge, or resources—doesn't deplete us; it multiplies our sense of fulfilment. When we give without expecting anything in return, we build networks of goodwill and trust, creating a ripple effect that touches countless lives. Generosity also reinforces our belief in abundance, reminding us there's enough for everyone. By lifting others, we don't lose anything; we gain a deeper connection to our shared humanity and a sense of shared success.

Abundance Is Limitless – The most liberating aspect of abundance is its infinite nature. When we embrace possibility, we realise that the only limits are the ones we impose on ourselves. This perspective encourages us to dream big, take risks, and pursue our aspirations without fear of running out—of time, energy, or opportunities. An abundant mindset rejects the idea of competition as a zero-sum game. Instead, it sees success as something that grows exponentially when pursued collaboratively. By believing in the boundless potential within ourselves and the world, we unlock the courage to explore new paths, innovate, and create a meaningful life.

When these principles come together, they create a life-altering perspective—a way of seeing the world not as a series of limits but as a landscape of endless possibilities. Embracing abundance is more than a mindset shift; it's a transformative approach to living, enabling us to thrive, contribute, and inspire.

The perspective of abundance is transformative. It allows us to shift from a mindset of fear and limitation to one of gratitude, possibility, and growth. By cultivating an abundant outlook, we can confidently navigate life's challenges and build a future rich in opportunity and fulfilment.

Abundance is not about having more—it's about being more. We make a choice every day to see the world through a lens of gratitude, generosity, and infinite potential.

Chapter 5

The Perspective of Lack

Lack is a force that quietly yet profoundly shapes the trajectory of our lives. It influences how we make decisions, perceive opportunities, and interact with those around us. It is not merely the absence of something tangible; it is a deeply ingrained perception of insufficiency. This mindset is more than a fleeting feeling—it can become a framework for how we interpret the world. When we see lack everywhere we turn, it creates invisible boundaries that confine our potential and limit our ability to embrace growth and fulfilment.

At its core, the perspective of lack is rooted in scarcity. It whispers that there is never enough—enough time, money, resources, or love. It fuels self-doubt, comparison, and fear, leaving us trapped in dissatisfaction and striving. But what if lack is less about external circumstances and more about the lens through which we view them? What if, by shifting that lens, we could unlock an entirely new way of experiencing life— one filled with opportunity, resilience, and abundance?

This chapter will delve into the complex layers of lack and how they affect our mindset, behaviour, and relationships. Lack isn't confined to material possessions; it can manifest emotionally, influencing how we value ourselves and connect with others. It can appear in societal constructs, shaping how communities and cultures view success, wealth, and happiness.

By understanding how lack operates, we can dismantle its power over us.

This journey will take us through the different forms of lack—real, perceived, emotional, and societal. We will examine how it can be a barrier to progress and a catalyst for self-awareness and transformation. Through stories, insights, and practical strategies, we'll uncover how to recognise and challenge the perspective of lack, reframing it to focus on what is possible.

Lack, like abundance, is not an unchangeable truth – it is a state of mind. And when we choose to shift that state, we gain the power to break free from the limitations it imposes. By the end of this chapter, you will have a deeper understanding of how to transform the perception of lack into a mindset that fosters gratitude, growth, and possibility. This shift is not just about having more; it's about seeing more opportunities, more potential, and more of the richness life has to offer.

The Parable of the Empty Cup

In a lively village surrounded by hills and fields, lived a man named Arjun. Known for his boundless ambition and relentless work ethic, Arjun was the embodiment of success—or so it seemed. He owned vast farmlands, managed a flourishing business, and was often sought after for advice. Yet, beneath this facade of achievement, Arjun was perpetually restless. No matter how much he achieved or acquired, he felt an unshakeable void, a sense that something crucial was missing.

One day, unable to ignore the gnawing emptiness any longer, Arjun sought counsel from a revered sage who lived on the outskirts of the village. The sage was known for his wisdom and simplicity; many travelled far and wide to seek guidance.

When Arjun arrived at the sage's humble hut, he explained his predicament. "I have wealth, success, and recognition, yet I feel unfulfilled. I work harder than anyone I know, but it never feels like enough. How can I find the peace and satisfaction I crave?"

The sage listened intently, nodding occasionally, and gestured for Arjun to sit. Without uttering a word, the sage began to prepare tea. Arjun watched, somewhat impatiently, as the sage meticulously boiled water, added fragrant tea leaves, and poured the steaming liquid into a small clay cup before him.

The cup filled quickly, but the sage continued to pour. The tea overflowed, spilling onto the table and dripping onto the ground. Alarmed, Arjun exclaimed, "Stop! The cup is full! Why are you still pouring?"

The sage looked up and smiled, his eyes twinkling with a knowing gleam. "This cup," he said, "is much like your mind. It is full of thoughts, worries, and an obsession with what you believe you lack—that there is no room for anything new. Until you empty it, how can you ever receive anything more?"

Arjun was taken aback, unsure of what to say. The sage continued, his tone gentle yet firm. "You see, Arjun, your life is overflowing with opportunities, blessings, and joys. But you are so focused on what you think is missing that you fail to see what is already present. You are like this cup, spilling over but blind to its richness. Empty your cup, and you will understand the abundance surrounding you."

The sage's words struck a chord deep within Arjun. He realised how often his thoughts were consumed by what he hadn't achieved, what others had that he didn't, and what might still elude him. Despite having so much, his perspective of lack had clouded his ability to truly appreciate and enjoy his life.

From that day on, Arjun began to approach life differently. He practised gratitude each morning, taking time to acknowledge the many blessings he already had. He stopped comparing himself to others and started celebrating his own journey. Slowly but surely, the restless void within him faded, replaced by a profound sense of contentment and peace.

This simple yet profound story reminds us how a perspective of lack can narrow our vision, trapping us in a cycle of dissatisfaction and missed opportunities. Just as Arjun needed to empty his overflowing cup to see clearly, we, too, must let go of the constant focus on scarcity to embrace the abundance already present in our lives.

We create space for gratitude, joy, and growth when we shift our mindset and stop fixating on what we don't have. It is not our circumstances but our perspective that shapes our experience of life.

Perspectives of Lack

The Lack of Resources

One of the most common perspectives of lack is tied to material resources—money, time, or opportunities. This mindset often stems from comparing oneself to others or focusing solely on limitations. A person who believes they don't have enough money might avoid taking risks and miss out on growth opportunities.

However, resource-based lack is often rooted in perception rather than reality. Take the story of entrepreneurs who started with nothing but a vision and built empires by focusing on what they could create rather than what they didn't have. The key is to shift focus from scarcity to creativity. Ask yourself: What do I have that I can leverage? What small steps can I take with what I already possess?

The Lack of Self-Worth

Another significant form of lack is internal – a lack of confidence, self-esteem, or belief in one's abilities. This perspective often results from past failures or societal pressures, convincing individuals that they are not "enough."

Consider how this manifests in everyday life: talented people may shy away from opportunities because they believe they're not qualified. This self-imposed limitation can create a cycle of missed chances and reinforced feelings of inadequacy.

Breaking free from this perspective involves redefining self-worth. Recognise that worthiness is inherent and not tied to external achievements. Practice self-compassion, celebrate small wins, and surround yourself with supportive voices that uplift rather than diminish.

The Lack of Connection

A sense of lack can also arise in relationships – a belief that one doesn't have meaningful connections or support. This perspective often leads to isolation, as individuals withdraw to protect themselves from perceived rejection or disappointment.

The irony is that this mindset perpetuates the very lack it fears. To overcome this, one must take small steps to nurture relationships. Vulnerability, empathy, and active listening are powerful tools for bridging gaps and building deeper connections.

The Lack of Vision

A lack of vision occurs when we are so focused on immediate needs or obstacles that we lose sight of the bigger picture. This shortsighted perspective can keep us stuck, unable to see the possibilities that lie ahead.

For example, someone stuck in a dead end job may feel trapped because they're focused on the limitations of their current situation rather than envisioning a path to something better. Developing a long-term vision requires stepping back, evaluating options, and daring to dream beyond immediate constraints.

Shifting from Lack to Possibility

To move beyond a perspective of lack, we must first recognise it. Awareness is the first step towards transformation. Ask yourself: Where am I focusing on limitations instead of opportunities? How can I reframe this situation to see what's possible?

Next, practice gratitude. Gratitude shifts the focus from what's missing to what's present. You create a foundation for growth and abundance by appreciating what you have.

Finally, take action. A perspective of lack often leads to stagnation, but even small steps can create momentum. Break tasks into manageable pieces, celebrate progress and keep moving forward.

Key Understandings of the Concept

Lack Is Often Perception, Not Reality – What we perceive as a lack is rarely an objective reality; instead, it is often a mental construct shaped by our experiences, comparisons, and societal expectations. For instance, people might feel they lack wealth because they measure themselves against someone more affluent, ignoring their financial stability. This perception of lack becomes a filter through which they view the world, creating a sense of limitation. However, shifting focus can reveal hidden opportunities and strengths. By reframing our perspective, we can recognise that what we thought was scarcity might be abundance in a different form. The key lies in changing the lens through which we see our circumstances.

Lack Breeds Fear, Abundance Breeds Courage – A mindset rooted in lack is fertile ground for fear—fear of failure, rejection, or loss. This fear often manifests as hesitation, avoidance, and self-doubt, preventing us from pursuing our goals or stepping out of our comfort zones. In contrast, a mindset of abundance fosters courage and resilience. When we believe there is enough—enough time, resources, opportunities, and second chances—we feel empowered to take risks, embrace change, and learn from setbacks. Abundance instils the confidence to move forward even in uncertainty, knowing that growth and fulfilment are always possible.

Lack Can Be Overcome Through Gratitude – Gratitude is one of the most powerful tools to counteract the mindset of lack. When we consciously focus on what we have—our health, relationships, skills, or simple daily joys—we shift our perspective. Gratitude redirects our attention from what is missing to what is present, helping us recognise the richness of our lives. It doesn't negate challenges or hardships but provides a foundation of positivity and hope. Over time, practising gratitude rewires our brains to naturally seek and appreciate abundance, making it easier to overcome feelings of lack.

Lack Shrinks Possibility, Abundance Expands It – A perspective of lack narrows our world, limiting our ability to dream, innovate, and connect. When we focus on scarcity—time, money, or talent—we become preoccupied with guarding what little we believe we have, often to the detriment of creativity and collaboration. On the other hand, embracing abundance opens up a world of possibilities. It encourages us to think beyond limitations, explore new ideas, and cultivate meaningful relationships. Abundance is expansive; it helps us see opportunities where others see obstacles, fostering a sense of hope and purpose that drives us towards a fulfilling life.

A perspective of lack may often seem like a trap that constrains our thinking and limits our actions. It makes us focus on what is missing and keeps us stuck in a cycle of scarcity. But the truth is, this trap is not permanent; it is something we can recognise, reframe, and eventually escape.

When we become aware of how the lens of lack shapes our worldview, we gain the power to change it. Reframing our perspective opens new opportunities, insights, and possibilities. What we once saw as an insurmountable obstacle can become a stepping stone to growth and success. The shift from focusing on what we lack to embracing what we have—what we can create and attract—can be transformative.

In this process, we realise that scarcity is not a given, and abundance is not something we wait for; it is something we choose to embrace. When we actively look for possibilities rather than limitations, our world shifts, and so do we. It's important to note that this shift does not mean denying challenges or pretending that difficult times don't exist; it means facing them with a mindset that sees potential in adversity, opportunity in challenges, and strength in the face of difficulty.

The key to overcoming the perspective of lack lies in recognising our power to choose how we perceive the world. We can choose to see abundance where others see scarcity and possibilities where others see obstacles. The journey from lack to abundance is not just about changing our mindset but reclaiming our ability to shape our reality.

As you reflect on the ideas shared in this chapter, remember that you hold the key to changing your perspective. The power to transform your experience lies within you.

Chapter 6

The Perspective of Relations

Relationships are the invisible threads that weave our lives together, connecting us to the world and the people around us. They are not just our interactions with others but the deeper, often unspoken bonds that shape our experiences, influence our emotions, and define our sense of belonging. Relationships are the foundation of how we navigate life, whether with family, friends, colleagues, or even strangers. They provide us with support, joy, love, and purpose while also offering challenges that push us to grow.

However, relationships are not static; they evolve and are constantly shaped by how we perceive them. How we interpret, value, and approach our connections can strengthen these bonds or create distance. Our perspective on relationships is pivotal in determining their quality, depth, and longevity. For example, if we approach relationships with suspicion, fear, or a scarcity mindset, we may withdraw or create walls that hinder intimacy. On the other hand, when we embrace relationships with openness, understanding, and a willingness to grow together, we foster deeper connections that bring us closer to those around us.

The lens through which we view relationships can influence every aspect of our interactions. Our trust, vulnerability, and communication beliefs shape how we relate to others. How we interpret conflict, misunderstanding, and emotional needs can build or break our bonds. But the beauty of relationships is that they are dynamic – they offer countless opportunities for us to shift our perspectives and evolve. The more we understand the power of perspective, the more we realise that we can cultivate healthier, more fulfilling relationships by simply changing how we look at them.

This chapter explores the concept of the perspective of relationships, offering insights into the different ways we can view and nurture our connections with others. It delves into the nuances of how we relate to people and the impact of our thoughts and attitudes on these connections. By understanding how our perspectives shape our relationships, we can begin to shift and realign them in ways that foster greater understanding, empathy, and intimacy. Through this process, we can build relationships that not only survive but thrive—relationships that enrich our lives and help us grow into the best versions of ourselves.

As we journey through this chapter, we will explore key elements influencing our relational dynamics, such as expectations, communication, boundaries, and emotional intelligence. We will also uncover strategies to help us see relationships through a lens of positivity and potential, allowing us to cultivate deeper, more meaningful bonds. By the end of this chapter, you will have a greater understanding of how to navigate relationships with a renewed sense of perspective, empowering you to create connections that are not only lasting but also transformative.

The Bridge Between Two Friends

Two childhood friends, Meera and Priya, lived in a village between hills. They had grown up side by side, their lives intertwined like the roots of the ancient trees surrounding their homes. They had been inseparable from playing in the fields as young girls to sharing their dreams and secrets under the vast starry sky. Their bond was deep, built on years of shared experiences and mutual understanding.

But as life often does, it pulls them in different directions. Meera stayed in the village, eventually taking over her family's farm, while Priya moved to the city to pursue a career. Despite the distance, they remained close, speaking regularly, reminiscing about old times, and offering each other support. Their friendship, though stretched thin by time and distance, seemed unbreakable.

That was until the day a disagreement over a family inheritance tore them apart.

It started innocently enough—an innocent suggestion about dividing the family property among the heirs—but quickly spiralled out of control. Old wounds were reopened, and emotions ran high. Hurtful words were exchanged, words that neither of them truly meant but were spoken in the heat of the moment. In the blink of an eye, the friendship that had once been unshakeable was left in tatters.

Meera, with her pride wounded, withdrew completely. Priya, equally hurt and feeling betrayed, did the same. Months passed without a word, and the rift between them grew deeper. Each of them, holding onto their hurt and their version of the truth, saw the situation through a lens of bitterness and defensiveness. They both felt they had been wronged, but neither could bring themselves to be the first to reach out.

One day, as the years continued to pass and the sting of the argument still lingered in both their hearts, Priya found herself sitting alone in her city apartment. The weight of the estrangement began to feel unbearable, and a thought lingered in her mind—could she fix this? Could she rebuild the bridge that had once connected them? After all, it wasn't just the inheritance that had caused the rift; it was the ego, the miscommunication, and the misunderstanding. It was the absence of empathy and the refusal to see beyond the surface.

With a new resolve, Priya made a decision. She would try. She wouldn't let pride be the final word between them.

Priya packed her bags and returned to the village. Upon reaching Meera's house, she stood on the edge of the small stream that separated their homes, staring across at the land where so many memories had been made. At that very spot, it was there where their bond had once been solid. But now, that same stream had come to symbolise the distance between them. With a deep breath, Priya made a decision. She gathered wood, stones, and whatever she could find, carefully constructing a small bridge across the stream.

It wasn't much, but it was a start—a symbol of her willingness to cross the divide, reach out, and make amends. When finished, Priya carefully placed a letter on Meera's doorstep. In the letter, she poured her heart out, apologising for the hurtful things she had said and done. She expressed her deep regret over their falling out and, above all, her desire to reconnect and rebuild the bond they had once shared.

The next morning, Meera stepped outside her door and saw the letter. Then, in the distance, she saw the small bridge stretching across the stream. A flood of emotions rushed over her. She was hesitant at first—pride, anger, and fear holding her back. But something inside her shifted as she stood there, looking at the bridge. Slowly, she walked to the bridge, her feet unsure but her heart open. Each step felt like a journey, a move towards forgiveness.

When Meera reached the other side, Priya was waiting for her, standing with her head bowed and eyes filled with apology. Without a word, they embraced, tears mingling with the warmth of their reunion. The years of distance, anger, and pain seemed to vanish in that moment. As they pulled apart, Meera spoke softly, "I've missed you."

"I've missed you too," Priya replied. "I'm sorry for what I said. I should have listened. I should have understood."

They both realised that the argument, the fallout, and the separation had been clouded by ego, pride, and misunderstanding. The way they had viewed the situation through their own limited perspectives had prevented them from seeing the bigger picture. But now, with open hearts and a willingness to listen, they could see it. They had allowed a simple disagreement to create a chasm between them, but now, by shifting their perspectives from blame to empathy, they could heal the wound and rebuild their relationship.

This story poignantly reminds us of the power of perspective in relationships. How we view and interpret conflicts, misunderstandings, and even the actions of others can either make or break our connections. When we view a situation through blame or ego, we create barriers that separate us. But we can bridge even the widest divides with empathy, compassion, and understanding.

Meera and Priya's story illustrates that not the disagreements or challenges in relationships define them; it's how we perceive and respond to them. Just like Priya did with the bridge, shifting our perspective can be the key to healing, forgiveness, and ultimately strengthening our bonds. Relationships, like bridges, can be rebuilt, piece by piece, when we are willing to change how we look at them and, in turn, how we approach one another.

Perspectives on Relations

The Perspective of Empathy

Empathy is the cornerstone of strong relationships. It involves stepping into another person's shoes, understanding their emotions, and responding compassionately. Many conflicts arise because we fail to see the world from the other person's perspective.

For instance, a manager who sees an employee's declining performance might assume laziness. However, with empathy, they might discover personal struggles causing the issue. By approaching situations with empathy, we create a safe space for open communication and mutual understanding.

To cultivate empathy, practice active listening, ask questions without judgement, and remind yourself that everyone has a story you might not see.

The Perspective of Reciprocity

Relationships thrive on balance—giving and receiving, sharing and supporting. When we approach relationships with the perspective of reciprocity, we recognise the importance of mutual effort and value.

Consider friendships where only one person tries to stay in touch or support another. Such one-sided relationships often wither over time. Viewing relationships as a two-way street fosters trust and longevity.

Ask yourself: Am I giving as much as I receive in this relationship? How can I show appreciation or support to those who matter to me?

The Perspective of Growth

Relationships are not static – they grow, evolve, and change over time. Viewing relationships through the lens of growth allows us to embrace these changes rather than resist them.

For example, as children grow into adults, the parent-child relationship shifts. Parents holding a controlling role might strain the bond, while those who evolve into mentors or friends foster a stronger connection.

A growth perspective involves being adaptable, open to change, and willing to learn from experiences within the relationship. It means acknowledging that relationships require continuous effort to thrive.

The Perspective of Boundaries

Healthy relationships require clear boundaries. While it may seem counterintuitive, boundaries create respect and trust, allowing relationships to flourish. Without boundaries, relationships can become draining or toxic.

For instance, in a work setting, overstepping boundaries by expecting colleagues to be available 24/7 can lead to resentment. Conversely, establishing clear expectations about work hours fosters respect and harmony.

Setting boundaries doesn't mean pushing people away; it's about protecting your emotional well-being while respecting others. Communicate openly about your needs and listen to the needs of others to establish mutually beneficial boundaries.

Shifting Perspectives for Better Relationships

Transforming relationships begins with one powerful tool: self-awareness. Without it, we risk remaining trapped in unproductive patterns, repeating old habits, and fostering toxic dynamics. So, take a step back. Reflect on your current relationships and ask yourself: What perspective am I bringing to this relationship? Understanding how your beliefs, experiences, and emotional triggers influence how you interact with others is essential. Are you coming from a place of openness, curiosity, and compassion? Or do you approach the relationship with judgement, defensiveness, or expectations that may not be met? By evaluating your perspective, you can identify whether it's helping or hindering the bond you share.

For example, when a person is locked into the perspective that their partner, friend, or colleague should act in a certain way—based on their values, desires, or past experiences—they inadvertently create a cycle of disappointment and frustration. Instead, stepping back and asking, "How can I better understand their point of view?" or "How can I meet them where they are?" opens the door to greater empathy, acceptance, and connection. Recognising that the lens you bring to the relationship can cloud or clarify your view of the other person empowers you to control how you shape the bond.

Once you've built that self-awareness, the next step is embracing a mindset of growth and improvement. Relationships are dynamic – constantly evolving as people grow, face challenges, and experience life's inevitable changes. So, it's essential to remember that no relationship stays static, and neither should you. If you want to improve or deepen the relationship, be willing to adapt your approach.

This means being open to learning from your mistakes, changing behaviours that no longer serve the relationship, and being courageous enough to apologise when necessary. Apologising isn't about admitting defeat; it's about recognising the impact of your actions on the other person and offering a sincere effort to right the wrong. Growth in relationships often comes from vulnerability and a willingness to take responsibility for your part, even when it's uncomfortable. This nurtures trust and shows you care about the other person's feelings.

Moreover, actively working towards strengthening the relationship is not a passive act. It involves consistent, intentional effort. Small actions—like listening without judgement, offering your time, or simply being present—can be just as powerful as grand gestures. Each day presents a new opportunity to contribute to the growth and depth of the relationship. Whether it's a romantic partner, a close friend, or a professional colleague, showing up with kindness, honesty, and patience builds a foundation for stronger bonds.

However, it's important to recognise that no relationship is perfect. The ideal of flawless communication, constant harmony, and total agreement is a myth. No matter how much effort we put into relationships, there will be misunderstandings, differences in opinion, and moments of tension. Instead of striving for an impossible state of perfection, shift your focus towards authenticity. Authentic relationships—built on mutual trust, empathy, and respect—are far more fulfilling and sustainable than superficial ones.

Authenticity in a relationship means allowing both parties to show up as their true selves without pretence or masks. It means acknowledging flaws, embracing imperfections, and accepting each other as human beings, not as projections of idealised images. When we approach relationships with authenticity, we invite others to do the same, creating a deeper connection. The beauty of authenticity lies in its ability to foster vulnerability and openness, which are the cornerstones of lasting relationships.

To cultivate authenticity, it's essential to let go of expectations of perfection and instead focus on mutual understanding and appreciation. Celebrate each person's unique qualities to the relationship and understand that conflict is a natural part of any meaningful connection. The ability to navigate those conflicts with respect, understanding, and a willingness to compromise allows relationships to thrive.

Ultimately, shifting perspectives in relationships is about more than just changing how we see others—it's about changing how we see ourselves within the relationship. Are you willing to grow, adapt, and put in the work needed to strengthen your connections? When you consciously choose to bring a positive, growth-oriented perspective to your relationships, you set the stage for deeper, more meaningful bonds that stand the test of time.

Key Understandings of the Concept

Empathy Is the Foundation of Connection – Empathy is the cornerstone of all meaningful relationships. It goes beyond simply listening to someone – it's about truly understanding their feelings, needs, and experiences from their perspective. Empathy requires that we step into the other person's shoes and momentarily see the world through their eyes, embracing their emotions as if they were our own. It's a powerful tool that fosters deeper connections and strengthens bonds because it shows that we care and are willing to understand, even when difficult.

When we practice empathy, we don't judge or dismiss the other person's feelings. Instead, we validate their experiences, which in turn builds trust. Trust is the glue that holds any relationship together, whether in a friendship, romantic partnership or work dynamic. The act of empathising with others can bridge gaps of misunderstanding and miscommunication, helping both parties feel heard and valued.

Empathy also nurtures compassion, the ability to feel for another person's pain or joy without immediately offering a solution or judgement. Compassion allows us to hold space for the other person, even in moments of vulnerability. It creates harmony, creating a safe emotional space where both individuals can be authentic without fear of rejection or ridicule. When empathy is present, relationships are grounded in mutual respect and care, allowing them to thrive despite challenges or obstacles.

Balance is Essential in Relationships – Healthy relationships are built on the principle of balance. This balance isn't just about equal effort; it's about reciprocal respect, understanding, and contribution from both parties. A relationship that lacks balance becomes one-sided, with one person carrying more emotional weight, responsibilities, or expectations than the other. This imbalance leads to resentment, burnout, and dissatisfaction.

In a balanced relationship, both individuals give and receive in equal measure. When someone gives too much without receiving it in return, they may feel unappreciated, exhausted, or unsupported. On the other hand, when one person is only taking and not contributing, the other person may feel taken advantage of or neglected. Both individuals must nurture and care for each other in ways that are equal in effort, respect, and time.

A healthy balance also involves emotional reciprocity. This means that both parties share their feelings openly and listen attentively when the other person speaks. It's about creating space for both voices to be heard, both emotions to be felt, and both needs to be acknowledged. When this balance is achieved, relationships become more sustainable, resilient, and fulfilling, with both individuals feeling equally valued and respected.

Change Is Inevitable and Necessary – Relationships, like people, are dynamic – they grow, evolve, and shift as time passes. People change, and circumstances change. This change can come from new experiences, personal growth, external challenges, or even shifts in values and priorities. Therefore, it's essential to understand that relationships are not static. What worked in the early stages of a relationship may not work years down the road, and that's okay. The key is to embrace change and see it as an opportunity for growth rather than a threat to the relationship's stability.

Approaching change with an open mind allows us to adapt to new circumstances while maintaining a healthy bond. For example, as individuals evolve, their needs, desires, and expectations within a relationship might change. A person may develop new interests, find new passions, or experience changes in their personal or professional life. These shifts may challenge the relationship, but they can also present opportunities to reconnect, communicate openly, and adapt together.

Embracing change allows relationships to thrive in the face of challenges. It encourages growth, exploration, and deeper understanding. When both people are willing to adapt and grow alongside each other, the relationship becomes stronger, more resilient, and more fulfilling.

Boundaries are Acts of Respect – Boundaries are often misunderstood as limitations, but in reality, they are crucial acts of respect in any relationship. Setting clear, healthy boundaries ensures that both individuals feel safe, valued, and emotionally secure. Boundaries are essential because they define where one person's responsibility ends and the other's begins. They provide clarity about what behaviours are acceptable and what are not, ensuring that both people's needs, feelings, and well-being are respected.

When boundaries are set and communicated clearly, they reduce the likelihood of misunderstandings or hurt feelings. Healthy boundaries also allow individuals to preserve their emotional and physical space, preventing one person from overstepping or demanding too much from the other. When both parties honour these boundaries, trust grows, and both individuals can operate from a place of mutual respect rather than fear of being taken advantage of.

In relationships, boundaries are not just about saying "no" to behaviours that are harmful or uncomfortable. They also involve recognising and communicating personal needs, desires, and limits in a way that strengthens the relationship. Boundaries encourage open dialogue, reinforce respect for each other's autonomy, and contribute to a healthier, more balanced dynamic. They empower individuals to take responsibility for their emotions and ensure that relationships are based on equality and understanding.

By recognising and respecting boundaries, relationships become places of emotional safety where both individuals can thrive without the fear of being overwhelmed, controlled, or dismissed. When set thoughtfully, boundaries pave the way for greater connection, deeper intimacy, and healthier interactions overall.

Relationships are the heart of human existence. They bring joy, support, and meaning to our lives but require effort, understanding, and perspective. By approaching relationships with empathy, reciprocity, growth, and boundaries, we can create connections that enrich our lives and the lives of those around us.

Ultimately, the perspective we bring to our relationships determines their depth and quality. View them through lenses of love, understanding, and possibility, and watch as your connections transform into sources of strength and joy.

Relationships are not merely connections between individuals; they are the very fabric of human existence. They shape our experiences, influence our emotions, and define our sense of belonging. Whether with family, friends, colleagues, or romantic partners, the relationships we cultivate can bring us immense joy, comfort, and support. However, like any significant aspect of life, relationships require intentional effort, understanding, and, most importantly, perspective. How we perceive and approach these connections is fundamental in determining their depth, quality, and longevity.

In this chapter, we've explored the essential principles that form the foundation of healthy, fulfilling relationships: empathy, reciprocity, growth, and boundaries. Each of these principles is a tool and a mindset—a way of viewing the world and our interactions with others. By practising empathy, we connect on a deeper emotional level, fostering trust and compassion. By embracing balance and reciprocity, we ensure that our relationships are sustainable and nourishing for both parties. Recognising that change is inevitable and necessary empowers us to evolve with our relationships rather than resist them. Lastly, setting and respecting boundaries creates emotional safety, allowing our relationships to thrive.

What stands out across all of these principles is the need for perspective. The lens through which we view our relationships will dictate how we navigate them. When we approach our relationships with love, patience, and understanding, we invite opportunities for growth and connection. When we view them through lenses of frustration, judgement, or scarcity, we risk limiting their potential and undermining the trust and joy that should be at their core.

Ultimately, the quality of our relationships is in our hands. We hold the power to choose how we show up for the people we care about, and it is in these choices that our relationships find their strength and beauty. When we choose to see our relationships through lenses of love, understanding, and possibility, we open the door to transformative, meaningful connections that enrich our lives and those around us.

Chapter 7

Perspective of Marriage

Marriage, often seen as the ultimate union of two souls, is one of life's most complex and transformative relationships. It is not merely a legal or social contract but an intricate tapestry of love, commitment, compromise, and shared dreams. However, how we perceive marriage shapes our experience within it. Is marriage a bond of duty or a partnership of equals? Is it a space of growth or a burden of expectations? The answers to these questions lie in the perspectives we bring into this sacred union.

In this chapter, we explore the perspective of marriage—how our understanding, expectations, and approach to this relationship determine its quality and longevity. We can uncover ways to create a fulfilling and enduring partnership by delving into diverse viewpoints.

A Story: The Potter and the Weaver

In a busy village, there were two artisans—Anika, a potter, and Sohan, a weaver. Both were proficient in crafts, creating pottery and woven items that the village residents appreciated. Their skills were notable, and they were also in a relationship.

Anika and Sohan dreamed of a life filled with love, prosperity, and the joy of creating together. They believed their marriage would be a perfect blend of their talents—just as a finely crafted pot holds the essence of the earth, and a woven fabric captures the stories of its threads.

In the early days of their marriage, everything seemed effortless. Anika admired Sohan's ability to weave intricate patterns without a plan, letting his hands and heart guide him. Sohan, in turn, marvelled at how Anika precisely shaped the most delicate clay pots, ensuring each curve was flawless. They inspired each other, and their differences felt like pieces of a beautiful puzzle coming together.

But as time passed, their differences, once a source of admiration, became points of contention.

Anika valued structure and careful planning. Every morning, she followed a meticulous routine—selecting the best clay, measuring the proportions, and crafting each piece patiently and carefully. She believed life should be lived the same way, with discipline and predictability.

Sohan, however, lived by the rhythm of inspiration. He wove his finest fabrics in moments of spontaneous creativity, letting patterns emerge as his fingers danced over the loom. To him, life was meant to flow like a river—unplanned yet purposeful, allowing beauty to emerge unexpectedly.

Over time, these differences created tension. Anika wished Sohan would be more structured and reliable, while Sohan wished Anika would loosen her grip and embrace spontaneity. Their once-harmonious conversations turned into heated debates. They spoke, but they did not listen. They loved, but they no longer understood.

One evening, as Anika and Sohan sat in silence, exhausted from yet another disagreement, an elderly woman from the village, known for her wisdom, approached them. She had seen their love blossom and noticed the cracks forming between them.

She invited them to her small hut, where two pieces of cloth were laid on the floor—one beautifully woven with intricate, colourful patterns, while the other was unravelled, with threads hanging loose.

She pointed to the first fabric and said, "Marriage is like a tapestry woven with the threads of two lives. Each thread is unique—one may be thick, the other thin, one bright, the other muted. Yet, together, they create something beautiful. If one thread tries to dominate the other, the fabric loses its harmony. And if neither thread bends to accommodate the other, the entire tapestry unravels."

Anika and Sohan looked at the second fabric, where the threads had failed to hold together. The elder continued, "A strong fabric is not made of identical threads but of threads that complement each other. Just as your crafts require balance—clay needs water and fire, and fabric needs structure and flow—so does your marriage."

The elder's words lingered in their hearts. That night, instead of arguing, Anika and Sohan spoke with open hearts.

Anika saw Sohan's spontaneity not as recklessness but as a gift—the ability to embrace life's unpredictability with joy. She realised that while planning was valuable, leaving room for the unexpected could bring new beauty into life.

Sohan, in turn, began to appreciate Anika's discipline—not as rigidity, but as dedication and care. He saw how her structured approach ensured their home and future were secure, allowing creativity to thrive within a strong foundation.

They no longer tried to change each other. Instead, they learned from each other. Anika allowed moments of spontaneity in her routine, trying her hand at shaping pottery without strict measurements. Sohan started setting small goals for his weaving projects, ensuring his creativity had direction.

Once on the verge of unravelling, their marriage became a beautifully woven tapestry that embraced structure and flow, planning and spontaneity, discipline and freedom.

The story of Anika and Sohan teaches us a profound truth about relationships: the way we choose to see our differences determines whether they divide us or strengthen us. Instead of trying to mould our loved ones into versions of ourselves, we can learn to appreciate their uniqueness.

When we shift from trying to change someone to understanding them, we create space for love to flourish. True harmony is not found in sameness but in the balance of differences.

Perspectives on Marriage

Marriage as a Partnership of Equals

The foundation of a strong marriage lies in equality. When both partners view each other as equals—equally responsible for decisions, equally valuable in the relationship—it fosters mutual respect and understanding.

In many relationships, one partner may unintentionally take on a dominant role, leading to resentment or imbalance. Shifting the perspective to see marriage as a team effort ensures that both voices are heard and both contributions are valued.

Practical Insight: Share responsibilities—financial, emotional, and household—and recognise each partner's unique strengths. Regularly communicate to ensure that one person's needs or efforts do not overshadow others.

Marriage as a Space for Growth

Marriage is often seen as a destination, but it's truly a journey. Viewing marriage as a space for personal and shared growth can transform how partners approach challenges and opportunities.

Every disagreement or obstacle can become an opportunity to learn more about oneself and one's partner. By embracing this perspective, couples can navigate rough patches with resilience and optimism.

Practical Insight: Cultivate a habit of reflection—individually and as a couple. Celebrate personal and joint achievements, and approach conflicts with the mindset of finding solutions, not assigning blame.

Marriage as a Union of Individualities

One of the most common misconceptions about marriage is that it requires partners to merge into one identity. While unity is essential, preserving individuality is equally important.

A successful marriage is one where both partners feel free to pursue their interests, dreams, and growth without fear of judgement. Viewing marriage as a union of two distinct individuals rather than a single entity allows for healthier dynamics.

Practical Insight: Encourage each other to maintain hobbies, friendships, and personal goals. Create a balance where togetherness thrives alongside individuality.

Marriage as a Commitment Beyond Emotions

Love is the cornerstone of marriage but not the sole foundation. Emotions can waver, but commitment sustains the relationship through highs and lows. Viewing marriage as a deliberate commitment rather than an emotional bond adds depth and resilience.

This perspective encourages couples to work through challenges rather than see them as signs of failure. It reminds us that love is not just felt; it's chosen every day.

Practical Insight: Reaffirm your commitment regularly, especially during tough times. Small gestures of appreciation and acts of love can rekindle the spark and remind both partners of their shared purpose.

Shifting Perspectives in Marriage

Transforming a marriage begins with self-awareness. Reflect on your expectations, beliefs, and behaviours. Are they nurturing the relationship or creating strain?

Next, focus on communication. Open and honest conversations can clarify misunderstandings, realign goals, and deepen connections.

Finally, embrace the journey. Marriage is a dynamic relationship that evolves over time. Adapting your perspective to align with its changing phases ensures the bond remains strong and fulfilling.

Key Understandings of the Concept

Equality Strengthens the Bond – A marriage thrives when both partners are treated as equals. Mutual respect, shared responsibilities, and value for each other's contributions create a harmonious relationship.

Growth Is the Essence of Marriage – Every challenge and achievement in marriage is an opportunity for growth. Viewing the relationship as a space for learning and evolving adds depth and resilience.

Individuality Enriches Togetherness – Marriage doesn't mean losing oneself. Preserving individuality alongside togetherness creates a balanced and fulfilling partnership.

Commitment Outlasts Emotions – Love is not just a feeling; it's a choice. Commitment sustains a marriage during emotional highs and lows, serving as the anchor in turbulent times.

Marriage is one of life's most profound relationships, filled with opportunities for love, connection, and growth.

By embracing diverse perspectives, couples can navigate its complexities gracefully, creating a bond that stands the test of time. When we approach marriage with empathy, respect, and a willingness to adapt, we unlock its true potential – a partnership that nurtures and uplifts both individuals.

Chapter 8

Perspective of Divorce

Divorce is often perceived as an ending, a painful rupture in the narrative of love and commitment. Yet, like any significant life event, divorce is not just an end; it can also be a beginning. The perspective we adopt about divorce is critical in how we process it, heal from it, and move forward.

Some see divorce as a failure, others as a liberation. For many, it is a mix of both – an emotional whirlwind that reshapes their identity and future. This chapter explores the perspective of divorce, revealing how a shift in mindset can turn it into an opportunity for growth, self-discovery, and new possibilities.

A Story: The Two Paths of Healing

Meera and Arjun had been married for twelve years. They seemed like the perfect couple – a beautiful home, thriving careers, and two wonderful children. Their friends admired their partnership, and their families took pride in their bond.

But behind closed doors, their reality was different. Years of unspoken resentments, constant arguments, and emotional distance had chipped away at the foundation of their relationship. What once felt like love had turned into exhaustion. Conversations became tense, silences grew longer, and both felt trapped in a cycle of unmet expectations and disappointments.

They had tried everything—counselling, self-help books, even brief periods of forced optimism—but nothing seemed to bridge the gap between them. It became clear that staying together was causing more pain than parting ways. After many sleepless nights and difficult discussions, they made the heartbreaking decision to divorce.

However, while the decision was mutual, the way they experienced and processed it was entirely different.

For Meera, the divorce felt like a personal failure. She had spent years investing in this marriage, believing that love alone should have been enough to make it work. She felt a deep sense of loss—not just of Arjun, but of the dreams they had built together.

She replayed the past, searching for moments where she could have done things differently. What if I had been more patient? What if I had fought harder? These thoughts haunted her, keeping her stuck in a cycle of self-blame and regret.

Beyond her internal struggles, societal expectations weighed heavily on her. Her family, though supportive, often reminded her of how marriages required "compromise and endurance." Friends who had once admired her life now tiptoed around conversations with her, unsure what to say. Meera felt isolated, defined by the end of her marriage rather than the years of love and effort she had put into it.

She buried herself in work to cope, trying to distract herself from the emptiness. But no promotion or professional success could fill the void left by her marriage's dissolution.

Arjun's Path: Embracing Change and Growth

Arjun, on the other hand, chose to view the divorce differently. He was deeply hurt, of course—letting go of a twelve-year marriage was not easy. But instead of fixating on what was lost, he asked himself, "What can I learn from this? How can I use this experience to grow?"

He sought therapy, not just to process the pain but to understand himself better. He realised that he had often suppressed his needs in the marriage, avoiding difficult conversations out of fear of conflict. He had been so focused on being the "provider" that he had neglected emotional connection—not just with Meera, but with himself.

With time, he began to rebuild. He strengthened his bond with his children, making an effort to be more present and engaged in their lives. He picked up old passions—music, hiking, and painting—things he had set aside in the busy routine of married life.

Arjun didn't see the divorce as just an ending; he saw it as a transition. A painful one, yes, but also one filled with opportunities for self-discovery.

Meera and Arjun went through the same event, but their perspectives shaped their healing journeys differently.

Meera saw the divorce as a collapse, a failure that defined her. She held onto the pain, believing it to be proof of her inadequacy. Her suffering was prolonged because she focused on the past and the "what-ifs" rather than the possibilities ahead.

While acknowledging the pain, Arjun chose to move forward. He saw the divorce not as an end but as a transformation. He allowed himself to grieve and made space for growth, learning, and new beginnings.

This story holds a profound truth: life's events do not define us—the perspective we bring to them shapes our reality. Divorce, like any major life change, can be seen as either a breaking point or a turning point.

We can view it as a permanent scar or a wound that heals into wisdom with time and care. We can choose to dwell in loss or embrace the lessons it offers.

Pain is inevitable, but suffering is prolonged when we resist change rather than grow through it. Like Arjun, we can shift our perspective—not to deny our emotions, but to see beyond them and recognise the possibilities that lie ahead.

Perspectives on Divorce

Divorce as a Catalyst for Self-Discovery

Divorce often forces us to confront who we are without the identity of a partner. This can feel daunting, but it's also an opportunity for self-discovery.

When a marriage ends, it strips away the roles and routines that may have defined us. This transition period can be used to explore personal values, passions, and goals. Many find clarity about what truly matters to them, leading to a more authentic and fulfilling life.

Practical Insight: Use the time after divorce to reconnect with yourself. Explore hobbies, seek therapy if needed, and set goals that reflect your aspirations.

Divorce as a Path to Growth

While painful, divorce often teaches resilience, patience, and self-compassion. It's a crucible that tests and strengthens our emotional endurance.

Growth arises from adversity, and divorce is no exception. It challenges us to face uncomfortable truths, process grief, and rebuild. Through this process, we often emerge stronger, more empathetic, and more aware of what we want in relationships and life.

Practical Insight: View setbacks not as failures but as lessons. Reflect on what the marriage and its end taught you about yourself and your needs in future relationships.

Divorce as a Liberation from Toxicity

For those in abusive or miserable marriages, divorce is not just an escape but a liberation. It is reclaiming one's autonomy, dignity, and well-being.

Staying in a toxic marriage can drain emotional and physical health. Choosing to leave is an act of courage and self-respect, allowing individuals to create a life free from harm and filled with possibility.

Practical Insight: Remember that walking away from toxicity is an act of self-preservation. Surround yourself with supportive people and resources that affirm your decision.

Divorce as a Redefinition of Relationships

Divorce doesn't just alter the dynamic between partners; it redefines relationships with children, extended family, and even oneself.

When approached thoughtfully, divorce can lead to healthier co-parenting arrangements, stronger individual connections with children, and a better understanding of personal boundaries. It also opens the door to forming new, meaningful relationships built on the lessons learned from the past.

Practical Insight: Focus on maintaining open, respectful communication, especially if children are involved. Prioritise their emotional well-being while navigating your new roles.

Shifting Perspectives on Divorce

To transform the way we perceive divorce, we must first let go of societal stigma and self-blame. Divorce is not a failure; it's often the healthiest choice two people can make.

Next, focus on healing. Embrace the emotional journey with patience, acknowledging the grief while seeking the opportunities it presents.

Finally, remember that divorce is a chapter, not the whole story. Life continues and holds the potential for new joys, connections, and growth.

Key Understandings of the concept

Divorce Can Be a New Beginning – Every ending is a beginning in disguise. Divorce offers the chance to start afresh, rediscover oneself and embrace new opportunities.

Divorce Teaches Resilience – The challenges of divorce teach emotional strength and adaptability. It's an opportunity to grow stronger and more self-assured.

Divorce Is an Act of Self-Care – Choosing divorce when necessary is an act of self-respect. It prioritises mental, emotional, and physical well-being over societal expectations.

Divorce Redefines Relationships – While it may end one relationship, divorce can improve others. It allows for the creation of healthier dynamics and the strengthening of bonds with oneself and loved ones.

Divorce is undeniably challenging, but it doesn't have to define us negatively. Adopting a perspective that focuses on growth, healing, and opportunity allows us to navigate its complexities with grace and emerge with a renewed sense of purpose and possibility. Life after divorce isn't just about surviving; it's about thriving. The perspective you choose will determine the path you take.

Chapter 9

Perspective of Money

Money is more than just currency – it's a symbol, a tool, and a mirror reflecting our beliefs, values, and emotions. For some, money represents freedom and opportunity; for others, it's a source of stress or even a measure of self-worth. How we perceive money significantly shapes our financial behaviours, relationships, and overall sense of fulfilment.

In this chapter, we delve into the perspective of money, examining the narratives we attach to it and how shifting those narratives can lead to greater abundance, financial well-being, and peace of mind.

A Story: The Tale of Two Friends

Vikram and Aditya had been inseparable since childhood. They grew up in the same neighbourhood, studied at the same schools, and even started careers in similar industries. To an outsider, their lives seemed almost identical. But beneath the surface, one fundamental difference was how they viewed and managed money.

Vikram grew up hearing stories of financial hardship from his parents and grandparents. His father often told him, "Money doesn't grow on trees. If you're not careful, you'll lose everything." These words shaped his financial mindset.

As soon as Vikram started earning, he became obsessed with saving. Every pay check was carefully divided—most of it went into his savings account, and the rest covered only the bare essentials. He refused to spend on anything that wasn't necessary. His old phone, despite malfunctioning, remained with him for years. He wore the same clothes until they were threadbare. Dining out, travelling, or investing in skill development seemed like unnecessary luxuries.

Despite having a stable job and a growing bank balance, Vikram never felt secure. He feared unexpected expenses, job loss, or a financial crisis. Even when opportunities arose—like investing in property, starting a side business, or taking a well-deserved vacation—he hesitated, convinced that spending meant losing control.

Over the years, his world became smaller. While his peers enjoyed new experiences, built relationships, and expanded their opportunities, Vikram remained stuck in a loop of earning and hoarding. He often found himself alone, his fears driving him further into isolation.

Though raised in the same environment as Vikram, Aditya had a different relationship with money. His parents had also taught him the importance of saving and emphasised that money was a means to a better life—not just something to be locked away.

When Aditya got his first job, he set aside some of his earnings for savings and investments, ensuring financial stability. But he also understood the importance of spending wisely. Instead of fearing expenses, he saw them as opportunities.

He invested in himself—enrolling in courses that enhanced his skills, attending conferences, and expanding his knowledge. He occasionally treated himself to enjoyable experiences, such as travelling to new places or dining at a fine restaurant. He also believed in giving back, donating to charities, and supporting causes close to his heart.

Aditya's mindset allowed him to take calculated risks. When he saw a business opportunity, he invested in it. When the stock market presented a good moment to grow his wealth, he made informed decisions. As a result, his financial standing improved significantly over time.

Unlike Vikram, Aditya never felt enslaved by money. He was financially stable but also emotionally content. He built strong relationships, experienced the richness of life, and never let fear dictate his choices.

Years passed, and Vikram and Aditya remained friends, although their lives had taken very different paths. One day, they met for coffee after a long time.

Vikram looked tired. "Aditya, you always seem so at ease with money. Aren't you ever worried about the future?" he asked.

Aditya smiled. "Of course, I plan for the future. But I also live in the present. What's the point of earning money if you never use it to improve your life?"

Vikram sighed. "I save so much, but I still don't feel secure. What if something goes wrong?"

Aditya leaned forward. "Something could go wrong, but it's about balance. Money is a tool, Vikram. If you let fear control you, you'll never truly live. But if you manage it wisely, money can give you freedom to grow, explore, and create a fulfilling life."

Vikram sat in silence, reflecting on his years of strict saving. He had thought he was being responsible, but had he also been denying himself the life he wanted?

The story of Vikram and Aditya highlights an essential truth—money itself isn't good or bad. It's our perspective that shapes our financial well-being and happiness.

Perspectives on Money

Money as a Tool

One of the most empowering perspectives is viewing money as a tool, not an end goal. Money is a means to achieve security, create experiences, and support causes that matter to you.

When money is seen as a tool, it loses its grip on our emotions. Instead of obsessing over accumulation, we focus on using money to enhance our lives and the lives of others. This mindset encourages intentional spending and a balanced approach to saving and investing.

Practical Insight: Create a financial plan that aligns with your values. Identify what truly matters to you and allocate resources accordingly.

Money as Energy

Money flows in and out of our lives much like energy. When we hoard it out of fear, we disrupt its natural flow, often leading to feelings of scarcity. Conversely, when we use money wisely and generously, we encourage a cycle of abundance.

This perspective doesn't advocate reckless spending but rather a mindset of trust. Believing in the money flow helps reduce anxiety and opens doors to new opportunities.

Practical Insight: Practice gratitude for what you have and embrace generosity, whether through charitable giving or supporting loved ones. Trust that money will flow back to you in ways you may not anticipate.

Money as a Reflection of Values

How we earn, spend, and save money often reflects our deepest values. Someone who prioritises security may focus on savings, while another who values adventure may spend on travel.

Understanding this connection can help us make financial decisions that align with our authentic selves. It also allows us to question societal norms around wealth and consumption, focusing instead on what truly brings us fulfilment.

Practical Insight: Reflect on your spending habits. Are they aligned with your core values? Adjust your financial priorities to ensure they reflect what truly matters to you.

Money as a Relationship

Many of us have relationships with money that are either fraught with tension or filled with neglect. Seeing money as a relationship invites us to approach it with care, understanding, and respect.

Just like any relationship, your financial health depends on communication (tracking your income and expenses), trust (avoiding impulsive decisions), and effort (investing time to learn about personal finance).

Practical Insight: Treat money as a partner in your life. Create a budget, set financial goals, and regularly review your progress to nurture this relationship.

Shifting Perspectives on Money

Changing your mindset about money starts with awareness. Ask yourself:

- What beliefs about money have you inherited from your family or society?

- Are those beliefs serving you, or are they holding you back?

The next step is to redefine your narrative. Replace limiting beliefs like "I'll never have enough" with empowering ones like "I have the resources to create a secure and fulfilling life."

Finally, practice mindful financial habits. Whether budgeting, saving, or investing, approach your financial decisions with clarity and intention.

Key Understandings of the Concept

Money Reflects Your Mindset – Your thoughts about money influence your financial reality. Cultivating a positive, abundant mindset is the first step towards financial well-being.

Money Requires Balance – Excessive focus on either saving or spending can create stress. Strive for a balanced approach that includes prudent saving, intentional spending, and meaningful investments.

Money Grows with Generosity – Generosity doesn't deplete your wealth; it amplifies it. Sharing your resources creates goodwill, strengthens relationships, and reinforces a sense of abundance.

Money Is Not the End Goal – While important, money is not the ultimate measure of success. True fulfilment comes from aligning financial resources with personal values and life goals.

At its core, money is a tool for living a meaningful life. By adopting a healthy perspective, we can move beyond the anxieties and limitations often associated with wealth, transforming our financial journey into one of purpose, peace, and possibility. Whatever your financial situation, remember: it's not about how much you have but how you choose to see and use it that defines your relationship with money.

Chapter 10

Perspective of Work-Life Balance

Work-life balance is often portrayed as an elusive ideal, a tightrope walk between professional success and personal fulfilment. However, the concept is far more nuanced than simply dividing our time equally between work and life. True balance lies in understanding priorities, setting boundaries, and aligning our choices with our values.

In this chapter, we'll explore the perspectives of work-life balance, discussing how these viewpoints shape our actions and attitudes. With the help of a compelling story, we'll uncover the challenges and solutions tied to achieving harmony between our professional and personal lives.

A Story: The Two Paths of Meera

Meera was a rising star in her corporate job. Her name was synonymous with success—she had climbed the corporate ladder at an impressive pace, earning the respect of her colleagues and superiors alike. Her calendar was always full, her inbox flooded with emails, and her phone constantly buzzed with notifications.

On the surface, she seemed to have it all: a high-powered career, a beautiful home, and a loving family. But beneath this facade, Meera was constantly exhausted. Her work consumed her time and energy, leaving her disconnected from her husband, young daughter, and—most painfully—herself.

One evening, as Meera rushed through dinner, half-listening to her daughter, Anaya, chatter about the school, the little girl's voice suddenly turned hopeful.

"Mama, my school play is next Friday! Will you come?"

Meera barely looked up from her phone as she responded, "Of course, sweetheart! I wouldn't miss it."

Anaya's face lit up with excitement, and for a brief moment, guilt pricked Meera's heart. She knew she had missed too many important moments, but she reassured herself that this time would be different.

But when Friday arrived, so did an urgent email from her boss. A critical last-minute meeting had been scheduled, and attendance was mandatory. Meera hesitated, glancing at the clock. If she left now, she could still make it to the play—but her boss's words echoed in her mind: "This is a career-defining project, Meera. We need you."

Torn between obligation and love, she sighed, typed out a quick apology text to her husband, and immersed herself in work again.

That evening, when Meera arrived home, Anaya was unusually quiet. Instead of running into her arms, she simply said, "It's okay, Mama. I know you're busy." Her voice lacked resentment, but the sadness in her eyes cut through Meera like a knife.

Something inside her shifted.

That night, Meera lay awake, staring at the ceiling, reflecting on her life. She had spent years chasing deadlines, promotions, and professional validation, but at what cost?

She saw two possible futures unfold before her.

The first path was the one she was already on: relentless work, more promotions, more professional success—but continued emotional distance from her loved ones. One day, her daughter would stop waiting for her. One day, she might find herself alone in a luxurious house, wondering where the time had gone.

The second path required a change. It wouldn't mean giving up her ambitions but rather realigning her priorities—learning to set boundaries, say no when necessary, and invest in the people who mattered most.

For the first time, she realised that success wasn't just about professional achievements; it was about fulfilment in all areas of life.

Determined to change, Meera consciously decided to take the second path. It wasn't easy at first. She struggled with guilt— guilt for stepping away from work at a reasonable hour, guilt for declining extra projects, guilt for prioritising her well-being.

But with time, she learned that balance wasn't about doing everything perfectly; it was about making intentional choices.

She started setting boundaries at work, ensuring her evenings were reserved for her family. She delegated tasks, empowering her team rather than micromanaging every detail. She rediscovered simple joys—reading bedtime stories to Anaya, enjoying long conversations with her husband, and even carving out time for herself.

The transformation wasn't immediate, but it was profound. Her work didn't suffer; she found that she was more productive and engaged when well-rested and emotionally fulfilled.

One evening, as she tucked Anaya into bed, her daughter whispered, "Mama, you don't miss the important things anymore."

Tears welled in Meera's eyes. That was the real promotion she had been seeking all along.

Meera's story reminds us that work-life balance is not a static achievement – it's an ongoing effort to align our time, energy, and priorities with what truly matters.

Perspectives on Work-Life Balance

Work-Life Balance as Integration

Rather than viewing work and life as competing forces, this perspective emphasises integration. It's about finding harmony by blending professional and personal activities to complement each other.

For instance, remote work arrangements allow people to spend more time with family while fulfilling job responsibilities. Similarly, hobbies and interests outside work can inspire creativity and problem-solving in professional contexts.

Practical Insight: Identify areas where your work and personal life can overlap constructively. For example, use family walks to brainstorm ideas or plan work goals during downtime.

Work-Life Balance as Prioritisation

This perspective emphasises the importance of identifying what truly matters. Balance doesn't mean equal time for everything; it means focusing on the areas that align with your values.

For someone building a career, work may take precedence during certain phases, while family or self-care might become the priority in other stages. Recognising that priorities shift over time helps avoid guilt and frustration.

Practical Insight: Regularly assess your priorities. Ask yourself, "What matters most to me right now?" and allocate your time accordingly.

Work-Life Balance as Boundaries

Setting boundaries is crucial to prevent burnout and maintain harmony. This perspective highlights the importance of saying "no" to tasks that drain your energy or detract from your personal well-being.

Healthy boundaries protect your time for relaxation, hobbies, and relationships. They also encourage respect from colleagues and loved ones, fostering mutual understanding.

Practical Insight: Create clear boundaries between work and personal life. For example, avoid checking emails during family time or designate specific hours for work-related tasks.

Work-Life Balance and Flexibility

Flexibility acknowledges that life is unpredictable. Sometimes, work demands more attention; at other times, personal life takes precedence. Embracing flexibility helps us adapt to changing circumstances without feeling overwhelmed.

This perspective requires self-awareness and the ability to adjust expectations. By remaining open to change, we can navigate challenges more effectively and maintain a sense of balance over the long-term.

Practical Insight: Develop a flexible mindset by practising mindfulness and adaptability. Accept that balance is not a fixed state but a dynamic process.

Shifting Perspectives on Work-Life Balance

Achieving work-life balance begins with self-awareness. Reflect on how you spend your time and whether it aligns with your priorities. Recognise the barriers preventing you from achieving balance, such as excessive workload, lack of boundaries, or unproductive habits.

Next, take proactive steps to create balance. This may involve delegating tasks, scheduling regular breaks, or seeking support from colleagues and loved ones. Remember, small changes can lead to significant improvements.

Finally, embrace the idea that balance is a journey, not a destination. There will be moments when work demands more attention and others when personal life takes centre stage. The key is to remain intentional and flexible in your approach.

Key Understandings of the Concept

Balance Is Personal – There's no universal formula for work-life balance. What works for one person may not work for another. Tailor your approach to align with your unique circumstances and values.

Balance Requires Boundaries – Clear boundaries protect your time and energy. Learn to say "no" when necessary and prioritise activities that nurture your well-being.

Balance is Dynamic – Work-life balance isn't a fixed state. It evolves as your priorities and circumstances change. Embrace flexibility and adapt to new challenges with resilience.

Balance Enhances Well-Being – A balanced life promotes physical health, mental clarity, and emotional fulfilment. It fosters stronger relationships, better productivity, and a greater sense of purpose.

Work-life balance is not about perfect equilibrium; it's about making intentional choices that align with your values and lead to a fulfilling life. By adopting a balanced perspective, we can achieve harmony between our professional ambitions and personal joys, paving the way for lasting success and happiness.

Chapter 11

Perspective of Power

Power is one of the most misunderstood and often misrepresented concepts. It is not simply the ability to control others or wield authority; true power lies in understanding oneself, influencing outcomes positively, and creating meaningful change. When approached with the right mindset, power can inspire, unite, and transform.

This chapter explores the nuanced perspectives of power, examining its role in our personal and professional lives. Through a compelling story and an in-depth discussion, we'll uncover how different viewpoints on power shape our interactions, decisions, and ability to lead fulfilling lives.

A Story: The Two Leaders

Two leaders emerged during a crisis in a bustling city amidst towering skyscrapers and a fast-paced corporate world. Their company, once a market leader, was now struggling to stay afloat in the face of an economic downturn. With dwindling revenues and mounting pressure from stakeholders, the organisation's fate rested heavily on its leaders and their ability to navigate uncertainty.

Akash and Priya were both entrusted with leading key divisions within the company. Both were competent, experienced, and driven. Yet, their approaches to leadership couldn't have been more different.

Akash believed leadership was about control. To him, power meant authority – the ability to make decisions, enforce rules, and demand compliance. In the face of the crisis, he tightened his grip.

He micromanaged every project, requiring constant updates and leaving little room for independent thinking.

He discouraged dissent, insisting that his way was the best.

He set aggressive targets, emphasising results over well-being.

When things went wrong, he blamed his team and sought scapegoats.

His team responded to his leadership with obedience, not enthusiasm. They delivered results in the short term, but they did so out of fear, not inspiration. Stress levels rose, creativity declined, and team members became disengaged. Over time, the cracks deepened—turnover increased, innovation stagnated, and despite their best efforts, their division's performance began to decline.

Priya had a different philosophy. She believed true power didn't come from control but from empowering others.

Instead of dictating every move, she trusted her team and encouraged them to take ownership of their work.

She listened actively, valuing diverse perspectives and making people feel heard.

She created a culture where failures weren't punished but seen as learning opportunities.

She shared successes with her team and took accountability when things went wrong.

Her team thrived. They felt valued, motivated, and personally invested in the company's success. They collaborated more, thought creatively, and found innovative solutions to help the company recover. While Akash's team operated in a climate of fear, Priya's team was driven by trust and purpose.

Months passed, and the company's fate became clear. Despite his relentless control, Akash's division struggled to sustain long-term performance. Burnout had led to mistakes, top talent had left, and the rigid structure had stifled adaptability.

Priya's division, however, thrived. They had discovered new ways to cut costs, optimise processes, and develop strategies that repositioned the company in the market. Their resilience and innovation played a key role in stabilising the organisation.

Eventually, the company's leadership recognised this stark difference. While Akash's style had yielded short term results, Priya's leadership secured the company's long-term survival. She was promoted to a senior leadership role, tasked with driving the company's cultural transformation.

Faced with the consequences of his choices, Akash had to confront a difficult truth: Power, when used for dominance, breeds resistance. Power, when used for empowerment, creates a lasting impact.

This story highlights a fundamental truth about leadership: True power doesn't come from authority but from the ability to uplift, inspire, and create positive change.

Perspectives of Power

Power as Authority

Many associate power with positional authority – the ability to enforce rules, make decisions, and command respect. While this perspective has its place, it often overlooks the importance of trust and connection.

Authority-based power can lead to compliance, but it rarely inspires commitment. Overreliance on positional power can alienate others, creating fear rather than respect.

Practical Insight: Positional power should be balanced with empathy, communication and collaboration to foster trust and loyalty.

Power as Influence

This perspective sees power as inspiring and guiding others without relying on formal authority. Influential power comes from authenticity, emotional intelligence, and the capacity to build relationships.

Leaders who embrace this perspective focus on understanding others' needs and aligning their efforts toward shared goals. Influence creates a ripple effect, encouraging others to contribute willingly and passionately.

Practical Insight: Cultivate influence by honing active listening skills, demonstrating integrity, and leading by example.

Power as Inner Strength

Power isn't just external – it's internal. Inner strength comes from self-awareness, resilience, and the ability to stay grounded in facing challenges. This perspective emphasises personal growth, self-discipline, and the courage to overcome obstacles.

When you harness inner strength, external circumstances sway your emotions and actions less. You remain calm under pressure, make thoughtful decisions, and project confidence that inspires others.

Practical Insight: Build inner strength through mindfulness, self-reflection, and practices that nurture mental and emotional well-being.

Power as Service

True power lies in serving others. This perspective shifts the focus from personal gain to collective benefit. When power uplifts communities, solves problems, or creates opportunities, its impact multiplies.

Service-oriented power fosters collaboration, trust, and a sense of purpose. It transforms power from a tool for control into a means of creating lasting, positive change.

Practical Insight: Use your abilities and resources to mentor, support, or advocate for those who need it. Power shared is power magnified.

Shifting Perspectives on Power

Our relationship with power often mirrors our mindset. If we see power as control, we may cling to it for fear of losing it. If we see power as a means of growth and service, we're more likely to use it responsibly and share it generously.

To reshape your perspective on power, reflect on how you define and use it. Ask yourself:

Do I seek power to dominate or empower?

How do I influence others?

Am I using my strengths to create positive outcomes?

Power is not inherently good or bad – it's neutral. Its value lies in how we wield it.

Key Understandings of the Concept

Power Is Responsibility – With great power comes great responsibility, and using power wisely means considering its impact on others and striving for outcomes that benefit all.

Power Is Amplified Through Sharing – True power grows when shared. Empowering others creates networks of trust, collaboration, and mutual success.

Power Requires Self-Awareness – Understanding your motivations, values, and strengths is essential to using power effectively. Self-aware leaders are less likely to misuse their influence.

Power Is a Tool for Transformation – When used with intention and integrity, power can transform lives, organisations, and societies. It can inspire innovation, foster unity, and drive progress.

Power, in its essence, is about potential – the potential to shape your life and influence others. By adopting empowering perspectives, we can redefine power as a force for growth, connection, and positive change. When wielded with wisdom, power becomes a tool for success and a foundation for meaningful, impactful living.

Chapter 12

Perspective of Religion

Religion has shaped humanity's journey for centuries, offering guidance, moral codes, and a sense of belonging. Yet, it is also one of the most deeply personal and often divisive subjects. For some, religion is a source of comfort and strength; for others, it may symbolise rigidity or conflict. How we perceive religion—whether as a path to enlightenment, a set of traditions, or a source of division—profoundly influences how we interact with the world and others.

This chapter will explore different perspectives on religion, each offering valuable insights into its role in our personal and collective lives. Through a poignant story and a detailed examination, we'll uncover how embracing diverse viewpoints about religion can lead to greater understanding, harmony, and self-growth.

A Story: The Bridge of Faith

In a thriving town between two prominent hills, there were two grand temples representing devotion and faith—one dedicated to the sun and the other to the Moon. For generations, the adherents of these temples remained separate.

The worshippers of the Sun Temple believed in discipline, action, and the pursuit of light, while the devotees of the Moon Temple embraced reflection, intuition, and the mysteries of the night. Though they lived in the same town, they rarely interacted, each convinced that their faith was the truest path.

One fateful evening, dark clouds loomed over the town. The winds howled, and rain poured relentlessly. The peaceful river that ran through the valley, connecting the two hills, swelled into a raging torrent. Bridges were washed away, homes were flooded, and chaos gripped the town.

The villagers on both sides were trapped with no way to cross the river. Food supplies ran low, medical help was out of reach, and fear spread like wildfire. Despite their devotion to their respective deities, the people found themselves powerless against nature's fury.

Amidst the despair, a young boy from the Sun Temple, Aarav, and a girl from the Moon Temple, Leela, took it upon themselves to find a solution. They were too young to carry the weight of prejudice that had divided their people for years.

"We can't survive like this," Aarav said. "We must build a bridge."

Leela nodded. "But we'll need everyone's help."

The task was monumental. The storm had left the land in ruins, and the river was still dangerous. But despite the challenges, the two children refused to give up.

Their determination sparked something in the villagers. Slowly, a few elders joined them. Then, more followed. Carpenters, masons, farmers, and even temple priests set aside their differences to rebuild what the storm had taken.

As the bridge took shape, so did friendships that had once seemed impossible. People who had once refused to speak to each other now worked side by side, driven by a shared purpose—not of faith, but of survival and compassion.

After weeks of relentless effort, the bridge was completed. The villagers from both hills stood together, gazing at their creation—not just a bridge of stone and wood but a bridge of understanding built with trust, kindness, and unity.

The temples still stood on their respective hills, their beliefs unchanged. But now, the villagers had come to a realisation:

The Sun and the Moon may shine at different times but are both part of the same sky.

Faith should never be a wall that divides – it should be a bridge that connects.

The Sun and Moon festivals were no longer celebrated separately from that day forward. Instead, they became a festival of light and harmony, where day met night, and people met as one community, bound by something greater than religious identity – their shared humanity.

This story reminds us that faith, when guided by compassion and unity, becomes a bridge rather than a barrier. Differences in belief should not divide us; instead, they should help us see the richness of diversity.

Perspectives on Religion

Religion as a Personal Journey

For many, religion is an intensely personal experience. It provides a framework for self-reflection, spiritual growth, and connection with a higher power.

This perspective focuses on how religion helps individuals navigate life's challenges and find meaning. It's less about dogma and more about personal transformation.

Practical Insight: Viewing religion as a personal journey encourages introspection and reduces judgement of others' beliefs.

Religion as a Cultural Tradition

Religion often intertwines with cultural heritage, shaping festivals, rituals, and community practices. This perspective sees religion as a way to preserve traditions, foster identity, and celebrate diversity.

However, when religion is reduced solely to tradition, it risks becoming stagnant or losing its spiritual essence.

Practical Insight: Embrace the cultural richness of religion while staying open to its deeper spiritual lessons.

Religion as a Source of Unity

Religion can bring people together, creating communities that support and uplift one another. Shared beliefs and practices can build solidarity and purpose.

However, this perspective can also lead to exclusion when the focus shifts to "us versus them." A unifying perspective requires inclusivity and respect for differing faiths.

Practical Insight: Use religion to foster understanding and connection rather than division.

Religion as a Philosophy

Some view religion as a collection of philosophies and moral teachings rather than divine mandates. From this perspective, religion guides ethical living, compassion, and wisdom.

This perspective appeals to those who value universal truths over ritualistic practices. It emphasises values like kindness, integrity, and service.

Practical Insight: Focus on the principles that align with personal growth and the well-being of others, regardless of religious affiliation.

Shifting Perspectives on Religion

Religion is multifaceted. Depending on how it's approached, it can be a source of solace, a cause of conflict, or a beacon of wisdom. Exploring various perspectives can redefine our relationship with religion and find common ground with others.

To shift your perspective on religion:

Reflect on your beliefs and their origins.

Engage with diverse faiths to understand their viewpoints.

Focus on universal values like love, kindness, and respect.

Key Understandings of the Concept

Religion Is a Path, Not a Destination – Religion provides guidance, but it's not the end goal. Personal growth, connection, and compassion are the true destinations.

Faith and Doubt Coexist – It's natural to question or doubt aspects of religion. These moments of introspection often lead to a deeper understanding and stronger faith.

Religion Can Unite, Not Divide – When approached with humility and openness, religion becomes a tool for building bridges across divides, fostering peace and harmony.

Religion is a Choice – Ultimately, how you view and practice religion is your choice. Honour your path while respecting others' journeys.

When understood as a multifaceted concept, religion becomes a tool for growth, connection, and enlightenment. By embracing its diverse perspectives, we can transcend differences and work towards a world rooted in mutual respect and shared humanity. Through this lens, religion transforms from a source of division into a profound force for unity and purpose.

Chapter 13

Perspective of Spirituality

Spirituality is often regarded as an elusive concept, a deeply personal journey transcending material existence. Unlike religion, which is often structured around specific doctrines and rituals, spirituality invites individuals to explore their connection to the universe, their purpose, and their essence. It is less about external practices and more about internal transformation. This chapter will explore the many dimensions of spirituality, understanding how different perspectives can reshape our lives and help us uncover a deeper sense of meaning.

A Story: The Lighthouse Keeper

In a remote coastal village, perched on a rocky cliff overlooking the vast, restless ocean, stood an old lighthouse. It had guided countless sailors to safety, its steady beam cutting through the thickest fog and fiercest storms.

Aarya, the lighthouse keeper, had tended to it for years. Every evening, she climbed its spiralling stairs, lit the flame, and ensured it burned brightly through the night. She took immense pride in her duty, knowing that the lives of sailors depended on that unwavering light.

Yet, as time passed, Aarya began to notice a peculiar pattern – the lighthouse mirrored her inner world.

On days when she felt strong and at peace, the flame burned effortlessly, its glow reaching far into the horizon. But the flame

94

flickered when doubt, fear, or sadness clouded her mind as if it, too, felt uncertain.

One evening, as dark clouds swallowed the sky and the wind howled through the village, a fierce storm rolled in. Waves crashed against the cliffs, and the lighthouse trembled under nature's wrath.

As Aarya checked the light one last time, she heard a frantic knock at the door.

It was Kavi, a village fisherman, drenched and shivering. His boat had nearly capsized in the storm, and he had barely made it to shore. Grateful for shelter, he sat by the fire as Aarya offered him warm tea.

As the storm raged outside, the two sat silently, listening to the howling wind and roaring waves. Then, Kavi spoke.

"The storm outside is like the chaos of life," he said softly. "But within each of us is a stillness, a light that guides us - if we learn to nurture it."

His words struck something deep within Aarya. For years, she had tended to the lighthouse's flame, yet she had never truly tended to her own. She realised that, like the lighthouse, she had been so focused on guiding others that she had neglected the light within herself.

That night marked the beginning of a transformation.

Aarya started waking up before dawn, sitting by the cliffs in quiet meditation, listening to the rhythm of the waves. She began journaling, pouring her thoughts onto paper, untangling the knots of doubt and fear that had dimmed her spirit.

She learned that spirituality wasn't about escaping the storms but finding the strength to shine through them.

She no longer feared the turbulence of life, for she understood that storms were inevitable. What mattered was keeping her inner light alive, just as she did with the lighthouse.

Over time, Aarya became a beacon—not just for sailors but also for the villagers. They noticed a change in her— a quiet confidence, a steady calm that radiated from within.

People began visiting her not only for the lighthouse's guidance but also for wisdom and the comfort of her presence. She would sit with them, listen, and remind them, as Kavi had reminded her, that the light they sought was already within them.

And so, Aarya continued her work, tending to the lighthouse and herself, knowing that true guidance doesn't come from a source outside of us—but from the steady flame within.

This story teaches us that our inner light is our greatest guide through life's storms. No matter how fierce the winds of doubt, fear, or hardship may be, when we nurture our inner stillness, we can shine through any darkness.

Perspectives on Spirituality

Spirituality as Connection to the Self

At its core, spirituality is a journey inward. It involves self-reflection, mindfulness, and understanding one's thoughts, emotions, and desires. This perspective emphasises aligning with your true self, discovering your values, and living authentically.

For instance, practices like meditation, journaling, or even taking long walks can help foster a deeper connection with oneself. This inner work often reveals profound insights about one's purpose and direction in life.

Practical Insight: Start with small acts of mindfulness, like focusing on your breath or spending a few minutes in stillness. These moments can help you uncover the essence of who you are.

Spirituality as Connection to Others

Another perspective views spirituality as a means of fostering empathy and compassion for others. It highlights humanity's interconnectedness and the idea that our actions ripple outward, affecting the lives of those around us.

This perspective inspires kindness, gratitude, and the desire to uplift others. It is often cultivated through service, listening deeply to others, or practising random acts of kindness.

Practical Insight: Engage in activities that connect you with others, such as volunteering or mentoring. These interactions often reveal the profound interconnectedness of life.

Spirituality as Connection to Nature

For many, spirituality is found in the natural world. This perspective emphasises the awe and wonder that nature inspires, reminding us of our place within a larger cosmic design.

Whether it's walking in a forest, sitting by the ocean, or gazing at the stars, nature offers countless opportunities to feel grounded and connected to something greater than ourselves. This perspective fosters humility and a sense of belonging.

Practical Insight: Spend time outdoors regularly. Observe the rhythms of nature and let them remind you of life's cycles and your own capacity to adapt and grow.

Spirituality as Transcendence

This perspective views spirituality as transcending the material world and connecting to a higher power or universal energy. It's about seeking meaning beyond the tangible and embracing the mysteries of existence.

For some, this might involve prayer, rituals, or studying sacred texts; for others, it might be about experiencing moments of awe and wonder that defies explanation. The key is to approach life with curiosity and openness.

Practical Insight: Practice gratitude and reflect on moments in your life that felt profound or transformative. These experiences often provide glimpses of transcendence.

Shifting Perspectives on Spirituality

Spirituality is not a one-size-fits-all concept. It evolves as we grow, shaped by our experiences, beliefs, and aspirations. To develop a spiritual perspective:

Cultivate a habit of self-reflection through meditation, journaling, or quiet contemplation.

Seek experiences that connect you to others through acts of kindness or shared rituals.

Spend time in nature to feel a deeper sense of belonging.

Remain open to wonder and mystery, allowing yourself to question and explore.

Key Understandings of the Concept

Spirituality Is Personal – There is no "right" way to be spiritual. It's a deeply individual journey shaped by your unique experiences and values.

Spirituality is Transformative – At its best, spirituality inspires growth, healing and a deeper understanding of oneself and the world.

Spirituality is Inclusive – Spirituality transcends labels and boundaries, reminding us of all life's shared humanity and interconnectedness.

Spirituality is Ever-Evolving – As we grow, our understanding of spirituality changes. Staying open to this evolution allows for deeper insights and richer experiences.

When embraced as a perspective, spirituality becomes a guiding light in our lives. It helps us navigate challenges, deepen our relationships, and find meaning in the everyday. By exploring its many facets, we unlock a profound sense of peace, purpose, and connection. Through spirituality, we discover not only who we are but also the boundless potential of the human spirit.

Chapter 14

Perspective of Hierarchy

Hierarchy is an inevitable aspect of human interactions, shaping how we work, live, and relate to one another. From corporate structures to family roles, hierarchies provide organisation and clarity but can also foster misunderstanding or inequality when not viewed with the right perspective. This chapter explores the concept of hierarchy, its different facets, and how understanding its nuances can lead to more harmonious relationships and personal growth.

A Story: The Tower Builders

The king announced an ambitious project in a grand kingdom where golden palaces shimmered under the sun. This towering monument would stand for generations, symbolising the strength and unity of his people.

He assembled the finest masons, architects, and craftsmen to bring this vision to life. Each worker had a designated role—bricklayers, stone carvers, sculptors, supervisors, and engineers. At the base of this structure, literally and figuratively, were the labourers mixing cement, carrying stones, and performing the backbreaking work necessary for the tower to rise.

Among them was Rajan, a young and ambitious labourer, full of dreams but burdened by resentment.

Rajan spent his days mixing cement under the scorching sun. His hands were calloused, his body ached, and yet no one noticed his work. The architect received the king's praise, the supervisors gave orders, and the sculptors created intricate designs that people admired.

As Rajan rested beside a pile of stones one evening, he vented his frustrations to an older worker.

"What is the point of working so hard? No one remembers the man who mixed the cement. They will only talk about the architect and the king," Rajan grumbled.

The older man smiled knowingly. "Do you think the architect's designs would stand without the foundation beneath them?" he asked. "A structure is only as strong as its base."

But Rajan was unconvinced. He continued his work half-heartedly, his resentment growing. His cement became weak, filled with small cracks—imperceptible initially but dangerous over time.

Months passed, and the tower began to take shape, its walls reaching for the sky. One day, as the king himself came to inspect the progress, he noticed something amiss.

Running his fingers over the structure's base, he felt tiny fissures forming in the mortar. Concerned, he summoned the architects and workers.

"This tower stands tall because of every hand that built it," the king declared. "But a single weak link can bring it all down. The smallest cracks in the foundation will one day cause the entire structure to crumble."

His gaze swept over the workers, settling on Rajan. "Who among you mixed this cement?"

Rajan hesitated, his heart pounding. Stepping forward, he lowered his head. "It was me, Your Majesty."

The king studied him, but his voice carried wisdom instead of anger.

"Every role in this kingdom has value. The tallest towers rise because of the strongest foundations. If the base is weak, the tower will fall—no matter how grand its design."

Rajan felt a profound shift within him. He had believed his work was insignificant, yet the king acknowledged its importance.

From that day on, Rajan took pride in his work. He mixed the cement with care, ensuring its strength. He no longer envied the architects or supervisors, for he understood that their work would be meaningless without him.

Rajan stood at its base as the tower neared completion, gazing up at the magnificent structure. It was a testament to every hand that had built it—every mason, every architect, every labourer.

And when the king inaugurated the tower, he did not honour just the architects and designers. Instead, he invited every worker, recognising that a great kingdom is built not by a few but by the collective strength of its people.

This story teaches a profound truth – a successful hierarchy is not about superiority but interdependence.

Perspectives on Hierarchy

Hierarchy as a System of Organisation

At its core, hierarchy exists to bring order to chaos. Whether in workplaces, families, or societies, it establishes roles and responsibilities, ensuring efficiency and accountability.

Perspective: When viewed positively, hierarchy is not about power but about clarity. Each level of the structure supports the others, creating a symbiotic relationship. For instance, in organisations, leaders set the vision, managers operationalise it, and employees bring it to life.

Practical Insight: Embrace your role and understand its value in the larger system. Focus on how your contributions support the collective goal.

Hierarchy as a Ladder of Growth

Hierarchies can also be seen as a pathway for personal and professional development. Moving up the hierarchy symbolises growth, learning, and the acquisition of new skills and responsibilities.

Perspective: Instead of viewing hierarchy as a rigid structure, see it as a dynamic ladder that challenges you to evolve. Each level you ascend brings new opportunities and perspectives.

Practical Insight: Approach every level with curiosity and a willingness to learn. Use your current position as a stepping stone to the next, cultivating skills and relationships.

Hierarchy as a Tool for Collaboration

While hierarchy often implies a top-down approach, it can also foster collaboration when roles and responsibilities are respected. Effective hierarchies enable people to work together seamlessly, combining their strengths to achieve shared objectives.

Perspective: Hierarchy does not mean inequality; it means interdependence. The success of any team or organisation depends on mutual respect and communication across all levels.

Practical Insight: Focus on building collaborative relationships with those above, below, and alongside you in the hierarchy. This approach strengthens trust and ensures collective success.

Hierarchy as a Reflection of Values

The way hierarchies are structured and maintained reflects the values of the system or culture they represent. A fair and transparent hierarchy promotes equity and inclusivity, while a rigid or exploitative one breeds resentment and stagnation.

Perspective: Hierarchies should serve the collective good, not just the individuals at the top. Leaders at higher levels should use their positions to uplift and empower those at the lower levels.

Practical Insight: Whether you're at the top or bottom of a hierarchy, uphold fairness and integrity. Advocate for systems that prioritise shared success over individual gain.

Shifting Perspectives on Hierarchy

Hierarchies can seem controlling or unequal, but with the right mindset, they can promote empowerment, collaboration, and growth.

Recognise the Purpose: Understand that hierarchies exist to provide structure and direction.

Value Every Role: Appreciate the contributions of every level in the hierarchy.

Seek Growth: Use hierarchies as opportunities for learning and advancement.

Foster Fairness: Advocate for transparent and equitable hierarchies that benefit all participants.

Key Understandings of the Concept

Every Role Is Important – No matter where you stand in a hierarchy, your contributions matter. Recognising this fosters respect and commitment across all levels.

Hierarchy Enables Growth – A well-functioning hierarchy challenges individuals to develop their skills and rise to new levels of responsibility.

Collaboration Is Key – Hierarchies thrive on collaboration, with each level supporting and complementing the others.

Values Shape Hierarchies – The effectiveness and fairness of a hierarchy depend on the values underpinning it. Leadership should focus on creating systems that empower rather than exploit.

When viewed with the right perspective, hierarchy is not a symbol of inequality but a framework for order, growth, and connection. By understanding its nuances, we can navigate hierarchies with grace, finding fulfilment in our roles and contributing to the greater good. Whether in professional settings, families, or communities, embracing a positive perspective of hierarchy enables us to build stronger, more harmonious relationships and achieve shared success.

Chapter 15

Perspective of Competition

Competition is integral to life, influencing our personal, professional, and social journeys. It can inspire growth and innovation but also breed envy and burnout when misinterpreted. How we perceive competition significantly shapes its impact on our lives. This chapter delves into different perspectives of competition, revealing how it can be harnessed as a tool for self-improvement, collaboration, and achievement.

A Story: The Race to the Summit

In a town surrounded by a towering mountain, two ambitious climbers, Aarav and Vikram, set out to conquer its summit. Both had trained for years, honing their skills, yet their mindsets towards the climb—and success—were vastly different.

Aarav saw the climb as a race to be won. He measured success in speed and superiority, fixating on outpacing Vikram.

"Only the first to reach the top truly matters," he muttered, tightening his gear.

From the moment they started, Aarav moved aggressively, leaping over boulders, refusing to rest, and dismissing anything that slowed him down. Every time Vikram paused—to steady his breath, admire the view, or help another climber—Aarav scoffed.

"You're wasting time," he called over his shoulder, pushing himself harder.

But with every hurried step, his energy drained, his muscles burned, and his focus blurred. He ignored his growing fatigue, determined to beat Vikram at all costs.

Vikram, on the other hand, viewed the climb differently. He welcomed the challenge but didn't see Aarav as an enemy—only as a benchmark to test his own limits.

"Reaching the top is important, but how I get there matters just as much," he thought.

When his legs grew weary, he took short breaks. He studied the terrain, choosing his steps wisely. When he noticed a fellow climber struggling with a slipping backpack, he offered a hand, knowing that helping others didn't slow him down—it strengthened him.

As they navigated a steep incline, Aarav's foot slipped on a loose rock. He stumbled, barely catching himself.

Vikram, despite being behind, reached out instinctively.

"We're both here to reach the top," he said, offering his hand. "Let's help each other."

Aarav hesitated—pride pulling him back—but exhaustion forced him to accept the help.

As the climb stretched into the final leg, Aarav's exhaustion overwhelmed him. He had spent all his energy in haste, leaving himself weak when he needed strength the most. His body screamed for rest, but the summit seemed so far away.

Vikram, however, remained steady, energised, and focused. He had paced himself, balanced effort with rest, and shared resources with others. Step by step, he climbed the final stretch and reached the peak first—strong, fulfilled, and at peace.

When Aarav finally arrived, he collapsed, panting. He had been so obsessed with beating Vikram that he had ignored the journey itself.

Looking around, he saw Vikram standing at the summit, not with the look of a victor over an opponent but of someone who had truly conquered the mountain—and himself.

Aarav realised a deep truth:

Competition is powerful, but focusing solely on it can hinder success and fulfilment. The best climbers pace themselves, help others, and respect their journey. Winning is not just about reaching the top but how you get there.

As they stood together, looking down at the vast world below, Aarav finally smiled.

"Next time," he said, "I'll climb smarter, not just faster."

And Vikram, with a knowing nod, replied, "That's the real victory."

Perspectives on Competition

Competition as a Catalyst for Growth

Competition can motivate us to strive for excellence. Setting a benchmark challenges us to push beyond our comfort zones and explore our potential. Instead of fearing competition, view it as an opportunity to learn and grow. Competing with others often reveals areas for improvement and inspires innovation.

Practical Insight: Focus on self-improvement rather than solely on outperforming others. Use competition as a mirror to reflect your strengths and weaknesses.

Competition as Collaboration

While competition often implies rivalry, it can also foster collaboration. Healthy competition encourages shared learning, where competitors uplift each other to achieve collective success. Instead of seeing competitors as adversaries, consider them allies in a shared journey. Collaboration within competition can lead to mutually beneficial outcomes.

Practical Insight: Look for opportunities to cooperate with competitors. Sharing insights and resources can create a win-win situation and foster long-term relationships.

Competition with Self

The most transformative competition is the one we have with ourselves. Striving to be better than we were yesterday fosters continuous growth and self-mastery. Competing with yourself eliminates envy and comparison, focusing instead on personal progress. It shifts the emphasis from external validation to internal satisfaction.

Practical Insight: Set personal benchmarks and celebrate small victories. Track your progress over time and aim to surpass your own achievements rather than others'.

Competition as a Mindset

How we perceive competition influences its effects on our well-being. A scarcity mindset sees competition as a battle for limited resources, breeding stress and resentment. An abundance mindset, however, views competition as an avenue for mutual growth and innovation. Adopt an abundance mindset to view competition as an enriching experience. Recognise that success is not finite—there's enough for everyone.

Practical Insight: Shift your focus from "winning at all costs" to "growing through the process." Appreciate others' success as inspiration rather than a threat.

Shifting Perspectives on Competition

From Rivalry to Respect: See competitors as individuals with unique strengths and challenges. Respect their journey while focusing on your own.

From Scarcity to Abundance: Recognise success is not a zero-sum game. Someone else's win doesn't equate to your loss.

From Stress to Motivation: Use competition as a motivator rather than a source of anxiety. Channel its energy into productive actions.

From Outcome to Process: Value the journey and the lessons learned over the result. Growth often lies in the experience, not just the achievement.

Key Understandings of the Concept

Competition Is a Mirror – It reflects your strengths, weaknesses, and potential. Use it to gain insights about yourself and strive for personal growth.

Healthy Competition Builds Connections – When approached with mutual respect, competition can foster collaboration and create support networks and shared success.

The True Rival Is Within – The most meaningful competition is against your own limitations and past achievements. Strive to outdo yourself, not others.

Mindset Shapes Competition – Your perspective determines whether competition fuels growth or breeds resentment. Embrace an abundance mindset to unlock its transformative power.

When understood and approached wisely, competition can be a powerful force for growth, innovation, and connection. By shifting your perspective, you can transform competition from a source of stress into an opportunity for learning and self-improvement. Whether in personal goals or professional endeavours, adopting a healthy approach to competition enables you to thrive without losing sight of your values and well-being.

Like the climber in the story, aim not just to reach the summit but to enjoy and learn from the journey. In doing so, you'll find that the true reward lies not in outpacing others but in becoming the best version of yourself.

Chapter 16

Perspective of Emotions

Emotions are a fundamental part of being human. They shape our experiences, influence our decisions, and affect how we connect with others. Yet, our emotions are often unpredictable and can be challenging to navigate. How we perceive our emotions and how we choose to respond to them determines the quality of our lives and our overall well-being.

This chapter explores the "perspective of emotions." We'll examine how our perception of emotions can empower or limit us and how changing our view can lead to growth, self-awareness, and resilience. By understanding different perspectives, we'll see how emotions can be tools for personal transformation.

A Story: The Storm Within

Priya had always believed that strength meant control—control over her emotions, thoughts, and reactions. She had spent years bottling up her feelings, pushing aside sadness, ignoring anger, and masking disappointment with a forced smile.

"Emotions make you weak," she told herself. "They cloud judgement. They distract you from what needs to be done."

But no matter how hard she tried to suppress them, her emotions grew stronger, surfacing in unexpected ways—restless nights, sudden outbursts, moments of deep loneliness. She felt like a dam struggling to hold back a powerful flood.

One evening, weighed down by an unshakeable sadness, Priya wandered through her village until she reached the riverbank. There, she noticed an old woman, known for her wisdom, sitting on a rock, watching the water flow.

Seeing the trouble in Priya's eyes, the woman patted the space beside her.

"Come, child. Tell me what burdens you."

At first, Priya hesitated. But something about the old woman's gentle presence made her feel safe. She sat down and spoke her truth for the first time in a long while.

She spoke of her frustration—how she tried so hard to be composed, yet inside, she felt like a storm was raging. She feared losing control and wished she could simply turn off the emotions that made life so difficult.

The old woman listened without interruption, her gaze never leaving the river. Then she said, "Priya, emotions are like this river. Sometimes, it is calm and smooth, reflecting the sky like a mirror. Other times, after a storm, it overflows, crashing against the banks."

She picked up a small leaf and dropped it into the water.

"See how the leaf flows with the river? It doesn't resist. It doesn't sink. It lets the river carry it forward."

Priya watched the leaf dance upon the water, gliding effortlessly with the current.

"But what if the storm doesn't pass? What if I get lost in it?" she asked, her voice barely above a whisper.

The old woman smiled, her eyes twinkling with understanding. "Storms always pass, child. They may feel endless when you are in the middle of them, but they never stay forever. And you are not the storm. You are the sky that holds it."

That night, Priya lay in bed, thinking about the river, the storm, and the sky.

For the first time, she didn't try to push away her emotions. She let herself feel. She allowed sadness to sit beside her. She acknowledged her frustration instead of drowning it in distractions.

She realised something powerful: Emotions were not the enemy. They were messengers.

Sadness reminded her of what she valued. Anger showed her where boundaries had been crossed. Fear pointed to where she needed courage.

By listening to her emotions rather than suppressing them, she discovered a sense of inner peace she had never known before.

Over time, Priya became more attuned to herself. Whenever emotions arose, she no longer saw them as threats but as gentle waves in the vast river of her mind—always moving, always changing, but never powerful enough to drown her.

She was not the storm. She was the sky.

Understanding Emotions: A Lens of Experience

Emotions are often misunderstood or dismissed in our society. From a young age, we are taught to manage our feelings—"Don't cry," "Don't be angry," "Keep calm"—as though emotions themselves are something to be ashamed of or avoided. This perception creates a complex relationship with our emotions, one where we feel the need to suppress or deny them to be accepted or "normal."

But emotions are not problems to be solved. They are experiences to be understood. They provide us with valuable information about ourselves and the world around us. When we shift our perspective on emotions, we see them as tools for growth rather than obstacles to our happiness.

Four Perspectives on Emotions

Emotions as Signals

One of the most empowering perspectives we can adopt is seeing our emotions as signals or messengers. Every emotion we feel—joy, sadness, anger, fear, or love—tells us something important about our internal world. When we are angry, it may indicate that our boundaries have been crossed. When we are sad, it may be signalling that we are grieving something that has been lost. When we feel fear, it could be pointing us towards an area of uncertainty or challenge in our lives.

Rather than trying to ignore or suppress these emotions, we can use them as indicators to better understand ourselves. By listening to our emotions, we open up the opportunity to explore what's beneath the surface—our values, desires, and needs—and take action that aligns with our authentic self.

Emotions as Temporary Experiences

Just as weather patterns shift over time, our emotions are not permanent. They come and go, often without us being able to predict when or why. This perspective is crucial for emotional resilience. When we recognise that emotions are temporary, we can step back and permit ourselves to feel without the pressure of forever holding on to that feeling. Instead of fearing or trying to avoid negative emotions, we can experience them fully, knowing they will eventually pass.

By reminding ourselves that emotions are transient, we can adopt a sense of acceptance, allowing ourselves to experience emotions without being defined. This helps us avoid becoming overwhelmed by our feelings and instead helps us regain control over how we respond to them.

Emotions as Tools for Personal Growth

Another perspective on emotions is to view them as opportunities for personal growth. Emotions often arise when faced with situations that challenge us, test our limits, or encourage us to question our beliefs. They push us to learn more about ourselves and the world around us.

For example, anger can be a tool for personal empowerment when we recognise it as a sign of injustice or unfair treatment. Sadness, though painful, can help us acknowledge what is important to us, prompting us to make changes in our lives. In this perspective, emotions become vehicles for self-improvement, growth, and transformation rather than being a hindrance. They encourage us to confront our weaknesses and embrace our strengths.

Emotions as Energy

Emotions are not only mental or psychological experiences but also energetic ones. When we feel emotions, they create physical sensations in our bodies—tightness in the chest when anxious, warmth in the heart when in love, a rush of adrenaline when afraid. This energy can either be constructive or destructive, depending on how we manage it.

By viewing emotions as energy, we can harness them for positive change. For example, instead of bottling up anger, we can channel that energy into productive activities, like physical exercise, creative projects, or advocacy. Similarly, excitement or joy can be cultivated to propel us forward, motivating us to take action towards our goals. Emotions, in this sense, become a powerful force for movement and transformation rather than something to avoid or control.

Key Understandings of the Concept

Emotions Are Not Good or Bad – Emotions themselves are neither good nor bad; they are simply responses to our experiences. Our judgement of emotions—whether we label them as "positive" or "negative"—shapes our response to them. Shifting our perspective to accept all emotions without judgement allows us to approach them with curiosity and understanding rather than fear or resistance.

Emotions Are Part of Being Human – Emotions are a natural and necessary part of the human experience. Trying to suppress or eliminate them only leads to frustration and disconnection. Instead, we can accept emotions as a core part of our being, acknowledging that they help us navigate our inner world and the external world we interact with.

Emotions are Powerful Tools for Growth – When we see emotions as opportunities for self-discovery and growth, we open ourselves up to personal transformation. Whether joyful or painful, each emotion carries valuable lessons that can guide us towards a more authentic life.

Emotions Are Energy to Be Harnessed – By recognising emotions as energy, we can choose how to use them. Rather than letting emotions control us, we can control how we direct the energy we create. This perspective allows us to be proactive rather than reactive emotionally.

The perspective of emotions is not about eliminating or controlling feelings but about understanding, embracing, and harnessing them for personal growth and transformation. When we see emotions as signals, temporary experiences, tools for growth, and energy to be channelled, we empower ourselves to live more fully, authentically, and with greater emotional resilience.

As you move forward, remember that emotions are not something to fear or suppress. They are part of who you are and serve as essential guides on your journey. By shifting your perspective, you can transform how you experience and respond to your emotions, turning what may feel like overwhelming forces into powerful allies for growth, healing, and self-discovery.

Chapter 18

Perspective of Life

Life is a journey. A series of experiences, encounters, and challenges form the fabric of our existence. Each day presents us with new opportunities to learn, grow, and evolve, yet how we experience these moments depends entirely on the perspective we bring. The way we view the world, interpret our circumstances, and approach the challenges we face can have a profound impact on our emotional well-being and overall sense of fulfilment.

This chapter explores the "perspective of life." We will discuss how perspectives shape our experiences, choices, and outcomes. Understanding this can bring clarity, peace, and joy. We will cover four life perspectives and provide tools to shift your mindset for a more fulfilling life.

A Story: The Two Paths of the Mountain

Nestled between towering mountains, a quiet village thrived in embracing nature's beauty. Two childhood friends lived in this village, Arjun and Ravi. Their bond had been unbreakable in their early years, filled with endless adventures, laughter, and dreams whispered under the stars.

As time passed, their paths diverged. Arjun became a successful businessman, his days filled with deals, deadlines, and a restless pursuit of more success, wealth, and recognition. His mind was always fixated on the future, constantly strategising his next move.

Ravi, on the other hand, took a different path. He became a spiritual seeker, dedicating his life to understanding the deeper truths of existence. He found joy in simplicity, seeking wisdom rather than wealth, and measured life not by achievements but by moments of awareness.

Despite their different journeys, fate brought them together once more at the foot of the great mountain.

The Legend of the Hidden Treasure

The village elders often spoke of a hidden treasure said to rest at the mountain's summit. Only those who braved the treacherous journey would find it.

Excited by the prospect of an extraordinary reward, Arjun saw an opportunity to add another achievement to his name. "This treasure must be worth everything," he thought. "Gold? Jewels? A fortune? Whatever it is, I will claim it."

Ravi, intrigued for different reasons, agreed to join the climb. He believed that the mountain itself had something to teach them.

The Journey Begins

Arjun surged ahead with the first steps of their ascent, focusing solely on reaching the top. Every obstacle – a fallen tree, a loose stone, a sharp incline – was merely an obstruction between him and his prize. "Keep moving, Ravi! We can rest once we have what we came for," he called back impatiently.

But Ravi took his time. He paused to breathe in the crisp air, feel the earth beneath his feet, and admire how the morning sun painted the valley in golden hues.

At one point, he stopped to help an old man who had lost his way, offering him water and a walking stick. Further along, he noticed a wounded bird and gently placed it in the shade of a tree. Each moment and step held its own richness, and Ravi absorbed it all.

Arjun, growing frustrated, shook his head. "You waste time, Ravi! The treasure is at the top, not in the dirt along the way!"

Ravi simply smiled. "Are you sure?"

Reaching the Summit

At last, Arjun reached the peak, his breath heavy, his muscles aching. He scanned the summit, expecting to find a chest overflowing with gold, a reward that would make his efforts worthwhile.

But there was nothing.

No gold. No riches. No tangible prize.

His heart sank. All this effort, all this struggle – for what?

Ravi arrived a little while later, his expression peaceful as he gazed at the breathtaking view. The valley stretched endlessly below him, the clouds danced around the peaks, and the wind whispered ancient secrets.

Seeing Arjun's disappointment, Ravi placed a hand on his shoulder.

"'The treasure, my friend, was never a thing to possess. It was the journey—the lessons, the moments of beauty, the wisdom gained."

Arjun, still unsettled, frowned. "But I worked so hard. I rushed, endured, sacrificed—only to find nothing at the end."

Ravi chuckled softly. "And yet, I walked the same path and feel richer than ever. Why do you think that is?"

Arjun remained silent, his mind replaying the journey. He had ignored the beauty around him, dismissed kindness as a distraction, and viewed every moment as merely a means to an end.

For the first time, he truly looked at the view. And in that moment, he understood.

The Shift in Perspective

The real treasure was not gold or jewels. It was a shift in perspective—the realisation that life was not just about reaching a destination but about experiencing the journey fully.

With a deep breath, Arjun sat beside Ravi, watching the world unfold before them. The mountain had given him something greater than wealth – it had given him wisdom.

And that, he finally realised, was the greatest treasure of all.

The Concept of Perspective in Life

Our perspective on life shapes everything we experience. It influences how we interpret events, respond to challenges, and perceive our purpose and potential. How we view our lives dictates the quality of our relationships, achievements, and personal fulfilment.

When we look at the world through the lens of our perspective, we realise that life is not just a series of events happening to us, but a canvas that we paint with our thoughts, beliefs, and attitudes. How we perceive ourselves, others, and the world around us will determine the experiences we attract and the opportunities we recognise.

Let's explore four powerful perspectives on life—each offering a distinct approach to navigating our existence.

Four Perspectives on Life

Life as a Journey of Growth

One of life's most empowering perspectives is seeing it as a journey of growth. In this view, every experience, whether positive or negative, is a learning opportunity. Life is not something that happens to you but something that unfolds for you. Challenges become lessons, and setbacks become stepping stones towards personal development.

When we view life as a growth process, we shift our focus from fixed outcomes to fluid learning. This mindset allows us to embrace mistakes, failures, and difficulties as part of our evolution rather than as signs of inadequacy. From this perspective, life is about becoming the best version of yourself—not by achieving a destination but by continuously growing, adapting, and improving.

Remember, Challenges are growth opportunities. Success is not defined by reaching a final destination but by your progress. Every experience, no matter how difficult, teaches you something valuable.

Life as a Collection of Choices

Another perspective of life is to see it as a series of choices. From the moment we wake up to the moment we go to sleep, we make decisions that shape our reality. Every action, thought, and interaction is a choice. Our choices determine our experiences, relationships, and the quality of our lives.

In this perspective, we acknowledge that while we cannot control every circumstance, we always have the power to choose how we respond. Life becomes about conscious, deliberate choices aligning with our values, desires, and goals. This perspective empowers us to take full responsibility for our lives, knowing that we are the creators of our experiences.

You have the power to choose your responses to any situation. Life is shaped by the accumulation of your choices, both big and small. Empowering yourself to make intentional choices leads to a more fulfilling life.

Life as a Dance of Impermanence

The third perspective we can adopt is viewing life as a dance of impermanence. Everything in life is constantly changing—our circumstances, emotions, relationships, and even our thoughts. This perspective teaches us to embrace life's fleeting nature and let go of the need for control.

When we adopt the perspective of impermanence, we learn to appreciate each moment for what it is without clinging to it or resisting its inevitable passing. Life is not something to hold onto but rather something to flow with. We become more adaptable, resilient, and open to new possibilities by embracing change.

It is important to note that everything in life is temporary, and change is inevitable. Embrace the flow of life rather than resisting it. Appreciate the present moment without worrying about the future or dwelling on the past.

Life as a Reflection of Inner Beliefs

The final perspective we'll explore is the idea that life is a reflection of our inner beliefs and thoughts. In this view, the way we perceive our mindset shapes the world. Our beliefs about ourselves, others, and the world at large form the lens through which we experience life.

When we see life this way, we recognise that our outer reality reflects our inner state. If we want to change our life experience, we must examine and shift our beliefs. This perspective emphasises the power of mindset and the importance of cultivating positive, empowering beliefs that support our growth and success.

As always, your outer world reflects your inner beliefs and thoughts. Shifting your mindset can transform your experience of life. Cultivating empowering beliefs leads to a more positive, fulfilling life.

Key Understanding of the perspective of life

Life Is Not a Fixed Destination but a Continuous Journey – Embrace the fact that life is a process of continuous growth, not a destination to reach. Every experience, every challenge, and every victory is part of a larger journey of becoming the best version of yourself.

You Have the Power to Choose Your Response – While we cannot always control our circumstances, we always have the power to choose how we respond. By consciously making decisions that align with our values and desires, we shape our lives.

Impermanence Is a Fundamental Truth – Everything in life is temporary—our emotions, situations, and relationships. By embracing the impermanent nature of life, we learn to appreciate the present moment and flow with change rather than resist it.

Your Mindset Shapes Your Reality – Life is a reflection of your beliefs and thoughts. By shifting your mindset and adopting empowering beliefs, you can change how you perceive the world and, in turn, transform your experiences.

Life, when viewed through different perspectives, becomes a rich and multifaceted experience. How we perceive our journey, our choices, the changes we face, and our beliefs about the world profoundly impact how we live. By shifting our perspective, we can find greater meaning, purpose, and fulfilment in every moment, regardless of the external circumstances we encounter.

As you reflect on these perspectives, remember that you can choose how you see and experience life. Embrace the journey, make intentional choices, flow with change, and align your beliefs with your desires. With the right perspective, life becomes a path of discovery and a canvas for creating the life you truly desire.

Chapter 19

Perspective of Death

Death is an inevitable and often unsettling part of the human experience. Yet, it is one of the few things we can all be certain of. For many, the idea of death brings fear, sorrow, and anxiety, while for others, it represents a natural transition, a part of life's continuous cycle. How we perceive death influences how we live and navigate our relationships, fears, and ambitions.

This chapter is dedicated to exploring the "Perspective of Death" and how our view of mortality shapes how we experience life. We will delve into four perspectives on death, offering insight into how shifting our perception can empower us to live more fully. By examining death from various angles—whether as an end, a transition, a teacher, or a release—we can begin to develop a more balanced and enriching understanding of our mortality. Along the way, we'll share a story illuminating the power of changing our perspective on death.

A Story: The Peaceful Passing of the Sage

Nestled among rolling green hills, where the morning mist wrapped itself around ancient trees, and the river sang softly through the valley, there was a small village. In this village lived Sage Devendra, a man of great wisdom whose presence was as steady as the towering banyan tree under which he often sat.

Devendra had spent his life guiding others and offering profound insights into the mysteries of existence. People from near and far came to him, seeking clarity on love, suffering, purpose, and the greatest unknown of all—death.

As the years passed, the villagers began to notice that Devendra had grown frail. His steps had slowed, his voice had softened, and a serene stillness surrounded him. His students sensed that his time on earth was drawing to a close, and though they did not wish to accept it, the truth lingered like an unspoken whisper in the air.

One crisp autumn morning, as the leaves gently descended from the trees, Devendra sat beneath his beloved banyan tree. His students gathered around him, their eyes filled with concern and sorrow.

Seeing their troubled expressions, he smiled, his eyes shimmering with unwavering peace.

"Why do you grieve?" he asked gently. "Death is not the end. It is merely a transition—like the changing of the seasons, like the river that never ceases to flow but only changes its course."

One of his youngest disciples, Amar, hesitated before speaking. "Master, how can you face death without fear? We cannot bear to lose you."

Devendra reached for a leaf that had just fallen into his palm. Holding it up, he said,

"Look at this leaf. It was once part of the tree, vibrant and green. But now, it's time has come to fall. Does that mean its purpose is over?"

The students remained silent, listening intently.

"No," Devendra continued. "The leaf does not die; it merely changes form. It returns to the earth, becoming part of the soil, nourishing the tree it once belonged to. In this way, it lives on, unseen but essential to the life that continues."

He paused, letting his words settle in their hearts.

"Just as this leaf does not fear falling, we too should not fear death. We return to the great source, to the essence from which we came. Our body may fade, but our essence remains, woven into the fabric of existence."

Over the next few days, Devendra continued to teach, his wisdom flowing like a river, preparing his students for his inevitable departure. He reminded them that life was a continuous dance of birth and renewal and that clinging to the physical only brought suffering.

"Do not mourn my passing," he said softly. "Celebrate the wisdom I have shared, for that is the part of me that will never die."

His words, though simple, planted seeds of understanding in the hearts of his students.

One evening, as the sun dipped below the hills, Devendra sat in quiet meditation, his breath merging with the rhythm of the wind. As his students watched over him, his body stilled like a wave dissolving into the vast ocean.

There were no cries of sorrow or despair in the village that night. Instead, there was a profound stillness, a quiet reverence. The people did not grieve, for Devendra had given them the greatest gift – a way to see beyond death and embrace the endless flow of life.

As the wind rustled through the trees, carrying fallen leaves to the earth, the villagers whispered his teachings to one another:

"Like the leaf that nourishes the soil, his wisdom nourishes our souls."

And so, Devendra's presence remained—not in the flesh, but in the hearts of all who had listened, learned, and understood.

The Concept of Death: A Universal Truth

Death is often perceived as the ultimate end, the cessation of life, the closing of a chapter. However, depending on cultural, spiritual, and personal beliefs, death can also be seen as a continuation of existence, a transition to another state of being, or a release from the burdens of earthly life. How we view death deeply influences how we approach living. Do we live in fear of death, or do we live in such a way that makes death seem like a natural part of life's journey?

Death is a concept that elicits strong emotional reactions, often rooted in fear and sadness. For many, it represents the loss of loved ones, the end of experiences, and the conclusion of all that is familiar. However, when we are able to shift our perspective and see death from different angles, it may help us understand that death is not as frightening as we might imagine. Instead, it can be a source of liberation, a teacher, or a reminder of the preciousness of life itself.

In the following sections, we will explore four distinct perspectives on death and how each of them offers a unique lens through which we can view our own mortality.

Four Perspectives on Death

Death as an End

The most common perspective on death is that it is the end of life. In this view, death signifies the termination of an individual's physical existence. Our bodies cease to function, and we no longer experience life as we did before. This perspective can lead to fear, anxiety, and resistance, especially when we think of our death or the death of those we love.

While this view is often seen as negative or distressing, it is also essential to the human experience. The awareness of death's inevitability can motivate us to live more fully, cherish our time on earth, and focus on what truly matters. The fear of death can drive us to seek meaning, purpose, and connection during our lives, encouraging us to leave behind a legacy or make an impact that transcends our physical existence.

Death represents the conclusion of life as we know it. The awareness of death's finality can motivate us to live with purpose and urgency. The fear of death can propel us to focus on what truly matters, such as relationships and personal growth.

Death as a Transition

In contrast to the "end" perspective, many cultures and spiritual traditions view death as a transition rather than an absolute conclusion. In this view, death is not the end of existence but a state change, a passage from one phase of life to another. Whether this transition is to an afterlife, reincarnation, or a return to the universe's energy, death is seen as a natural progression rather than a tragic end.

This perspective provides comfort and hope, as it suggests that death is not something to be feared but part of a larger cycle of existence. For individuals who believe in an afterlife or spiritual continuity, death is an opportunity for growth and exploration beyond the physical realm.

Death is seen as a transition to another state of existence rather than an end. This view often brings comfort, as it suggests life continues in some form beyond death. Embracing the idea of death as a transition can help us live without fear of the unknown.

Death as a Teacher

Death, when seen from a teacher's perspective, offers profound lessons. It teaches us the impermanence of life, the transient nature of our emotions and experiences, and the value of living authentically. By reflecting on death, we can learn to live with greater appreciation, mindfulness, and compassion.

When we confront the reality of our mortality, we become more aware of our priorities, desires, and connections with others. Death teaches us that our time is limited and that every moment matters. It encourages us to cherish the present, be more compassionate towards others, and let go of unnecessary fears, grudges, or attachments.

Death teaches us the impermanence of all things and the fleeting nature of life. Reflecting on death encourages us to live more fully and authentically. Death reminds us to appreciate the present and prioritise what truly matters.

Death as a Release

The final perspective we'll explore is that of death as a release—a liberation from the physical body, the struggles of the mind, and the limitations of earthly existence. For those suffering from illness, old age, or hardship, death may be viewed as a final release from pain, a surrender to the inevitable that brings peace and relief.

This perspective can comfort those nearing the end of their lives or those who are caring for loved ones. By accepting death as a release, individuals may find solace in the idea that death is a natural and necessary part of the life cycle, offering release from suffering and the promise of peace.

Death is seen as a release from suffering, limitations, and the challenges of life. Embracing death as a release can bring peace to those who are facing illness, old age, or hardship. This perspective encourages acceptance and peace in the face of mortality.

Key Understanding of the Perspective of Death

Death is Inevitable, But Our Response to It is a Choice – While we cannot avoid death, we can choose how we respond to it. By understanding death as a transition, a teacher, or a release, we can cultivate peace and acceptance in the face of mortality.

Life and Death Are Part of a Larger Cycle – Life is not a static experience; it is part of a continuous cycle that includes birth, living, and death. Embracing this cycle with grace allows us to view death not as a tragedy but as a natural transition.

Death Reminds Us to Live Fully – The awareness of death's inevitability encourages us to live more authentically and with purpose. It serves as a reminder that every moment is precious and that we must cherish our time here on earth.

Death Can Be a Source of Comfort and Peace – By shifting our perspective on death, we can find comfort and peace. Death is not something to be feared but understood as part of the greater journey of existence.

Death is a universal experience that touches each of us at different points in our lives. While it is often met with fear, grief, and resistance, there is immense value in exploring different perspectives on death. Whether we view it as an end, a transition, a teacher, or a release, each perspective offers insight into how we can live more fully and meaningfully.

By shifting our perspective on death, we can free ourselves from the fear and anxiety that often accompany it. Instead, we can embrace life's impermanence, live with purpose, and approach death with peace and acceptance. Ultimately, the perspective we bring to death shapes how we live—and how we live shapes the quality of our lives and the legacy we leave behind.

Chapter 20

Perspective of Completion

Completion is a concept that most of us have been conditioned to understand as an endpoint – a final result or conclusion. It's often associated with finishing a task, achieving a goal, or reaching a desired outcome. Yet, completion is not always as clear-cut as it seems. What does it truly mean to complete something? Is it simply the end of a process, or is there something more? Can we ever truly reach completion, or is it a never-ending journey?

In this chapter, we will explore the "perspective of completion" and how shifting our perception of what it means to be complete can have a profound impact on our lives. We will examine completion from four different angles and illustrate each perspective through a story that offers valuable insights into the nature of completion. Ultimately, understanding these diverse views can create a more holistic understanding of the concept and unlock a deeper sense of fulfilment and peace in our lives.

A Story: The Journey of the Potter

A potter named Arjun lived in a small village nestled along the banks of a gently flowing river. He was known far and wide for his exquisite pottery—each piece a masterpiece of form, balance, and artistry. His hands, weathered by years of work, moved with the precision of a sculptor and the grace of a dancer.

People travelled from distant villages to see his creations, admiring the delicate curves, the intricate designs, and how his pottery seemed to hold a quiet soul within its earthen walls. But despite his renown, Arjun remained humble, knowing that mastery was an endless journey, not a destination.

One summer morning, a young apprentice named Ravi arrived at Arjun's workshop. With eager eyes and calloused hands from past labour, Ravi had come to learn the art of pottery, dreaming of one day crafting pieces as flawless as his mentor's.

Arjun welcomed him warmly and began teaching him the ways of the clay – the balance of pressure and release, patience and precision, and the harmony between human intent and nature's will.

At first, Ravi watched in awe. Arjun's hands moulded the clay with an effortless rhythm, shaping it into elegant bowls, sturdy pots, and graceful vases. His fingers knew when to apply pressure and when to ease when to add water and when to let the clay rest.

Eager to prove himself, Ravi sat at the wheel for the first time. His hands trembled as he touched the spinning clay, and soon, his excitement turned into frustration.

The clay collapsed.

The pot wobbled.

The edges cracked.

No matter how hard he tried, his creation always seemed unfinished, imperfect, and incomplete.

Frustrated, he asked Arjun, "When will I know if the pot is finished? How do I know when it's truly complete?"

Arjun smiled, his eyes reflecting both patience and understanding. Placing a gentle hand on Ravi's shoulder, he said,

"Completion is not about reaching a final point, Ravi. It is not a single moment but a process. A pot may look perfect to one person, but it may seem unfinished to another. True artistry lies in understanding that completion is fluid—it is about knowing when to stop and that there is always room to grow."

Ravi frowned. "But how will I know when to stop?"

Arjun chuckled and led him to the shelves where rows of finished pottery stood, each piece different from the next.

"Look at these," he said. "Each of these pots has a different story. Some are adorned with patterns, some are smooth, and some have imperfections that make them unique. A pot does not have to be perfect to be complete—it only needs to serve its purpose."

Ravi gazed at the pots, running his fingers over their surfaces. He saw tiny cracks, uneven curves, and subtle colour variations—details he had previously dismissed as mistakes.

As Ravi continued his training, he began to see pottery in a new light. Each piece he created was not just an end goal but a lesson.

One day, as he carefully shaped a clay pot, he realised that completion is not about flawlessness but growth.

His pots became stronger and refined, but he never saw his work as "finished." Instead, he viewed each piece as a milestone on an ever-evolving journey of improvement, creativity, and self-discovery.

Years passed, and one day, Ravi found himself in the position his mentor once held—teaching a new apprentice who sat at the wheel, struggling just as he once had.

When the apprentice asked, "How do I know when the pot is complete?" Ravi smiled, his hands mirroring Arjun's gentle touch, and replied:

"Completion is not an endpoint – it is a step along the way. And the way never truly ends."

In modern society, we often view completion as linear: a task is finished, a goal is met, and the job is done. But the idea of completion extends far beyond this simple equation. In reality, completion is a multifaceted concept that varies depending on the context in which it is applied. While finishing a project or achieving a goal might signify one kind of completion, many other aspects—personal, emotional, spiritual, and relational—influence our experience of completion.

It's important to realise that completion is not always about reaching an endpoint; it's about how we engage with the journey. In many areas of life, the process is just as meaningful as the result. Pursuing a goal or completing a task may be seen as a stepping stone to something greater, something that continues to evolve even after we've crossed the finish line.

We often get caught up in the idea that completion means finality, but this limited view can leave us feeling unfulfilled or unsatisfied when we inevitably encounter new challenges or setbacks. Embracing a broader understanding of completion allows us to approach life with peace and acceptance, recognising that there is no "perfect" endpoint, only continuous growth and transformation.

Four Perspectives on Completion

Completion as an Endpoint

The most conventional view of completion is that it represents the end of a process—when a project is finished, a goal is reached, or a task is completed. This perspective is often associated with achievement and accomplishment. In our work, education, and daily lives, we frequently set out to finish what we start, whether it's a professional project, a personal goal, or an activity.

While there's nothing wrong with this view of completion, it can sometimes lead to dissatisfaction if the "end" doesn't meet our expectations. For example, after completing a large project, some may feel relief but soon realise that a sense of emptiness follows. They may have finished the task but don't feel fulfilled, and the next goal or challenge quickly takes place. This cycle can leave us perpetually chasing completion without ever feeling truly satisfied.

Completion is seen as the end of a task, project, or phase in life. This view of completion can be motivating, but it can also lead to feelings of emptiness if not coupled with a deeper sense of fulfilment. Completion can be fulfilling, but it's important to recognise that there's always something new to pursue.

Completion as a Cycle

Another perspective of completion is that it represents the completion of a cycle, after which the cycle begins again. Life follows cyclical patterns—day and night, seasons, and even the cycles of birth, growth, decay, and death. Similarly, many processes in life, such as learning or creating, are never truly complete. After one cycle ends, another begins.

For example, consider personal growth. We may complete one stage of self-development only to begin another stage with new challenges and opportunities. This perspective emphasises that completion is not about reaching a final destination but about recognising the stages and cycles of the larger journey. Each cycle may mark a sense of achievement or progress, but it is only a moment in the ongoing flow of life.

Completion is seen as the end of one cycle, after which a new cycle begins. This perspective highlights the ongoing nature of growth and transformation. Embracing cycles allows us to understand that life is not about reaching a final goal but continually evolving.

Completion as Integration

In some cases, completion is not about an outcome but about integration. It's fully accepting and incorporating lessons learned, emotions experienced, and wisdom gained from a particular experience. From this perspective, completion is a state of inner wholeness, a sense of alignment, and the ability to move forward without lingering attachments or regrets.

For example, in relationships, completion may occur when we've fully processed an experience—whether positive or negative—and integrated the lessons learned. This integration allows us to let go of what no longer serves us and move forward with peace and clarity. In this view, completion is about emotional and psychological resolution, rather than the mere cessation of activity.

Completion is about integration—fully accepting and incorporating lessons from an experience. This perspective emphasises emotional closure and inner peace. Completion leads to growth and personal development, allowing us to move forward with clarity.

Completion as Continuous Growth

Finally, completion can be viewed as continuous growth, where each achievement, no matter how small, is part of an ongoing process of self-improvement and expansion. This perspective rejects the idea of "finality" in favour of a constant state of progress. Completion is seen as a series of moments of growth rather than a singular event.

For instance, in the realm of personal development, completion is not about becoming perfect or achieving an ultimate goal. It's about consistently working on oneself, evolving, and expanding. From this viewpoint, we never truly reach "completion" because we are always in the process of becoming. This perspective allows us to embrace life as a journey and gives us permission to grow and learn continuously.

Completion is seen as a continuous process of growth and development. This perspective emphasises that we are always evolving, never truly "done." It encourages lifelong learning and self-improvement, fostering a sense of peace in the process.

Key Understanding of the perspective of completion

Completion is not Always an End – It's essential to recognise that completion isn't necessarily about finality. It can represent the end of one chapter, but it also signals the beginning of another.

Completion Can Be a Cycle – Many aspects of life, such as personal growth, learning, and relationships, follow cyclical patterns. Completion is just a pause in an ongoing cycle.

Completion Involves Integration – True completion comes when we've fully processed, integrated, and learned from an experience, allowing us to move forward with clarity.

Completion is Continuous Growth – Completion should be seen as an ongoing process of growth, where each step we take brings us closer to becoming the best version Sof ourselves.

The concept of completion is multifaceted, and how we choose to view it can significantly impact how we experience our journey. Whether we see completion as an endpoint, a cycle, an integration of lessons, or continuous growth, each perspective provides valuable insights that can enrich our lives. By embracing a more holistic view of completion, we can free ourselves from the pressure to reach a final destination and instead appreciate the process of becoming, learning, and growing.

In the end, completion is not something to fear or rush towards; it is something to embrace in all its forms. When we approach life with an understanding of completion that honours the journey, we find greater fulfilment, peace, and purpose in our everyday lives.

Chapter 21

Perspective of Reality

Reality is often seen as something concrete and unchangeable. Yet, reality, as we experience it, is not an objective truth but rather a subjective experience—shaped and influenced by our perceptions, beliefs, and emotions. The way we view the world around us can either limit us or expand the possibilities we encounter. Our reality is shaped by the lenses we wear, which can be changed. Shifting your perspective on reality is one of the most powerful tools for personal growth and transformation. It allows you to break free from limitations and open your mind to new possibilities, growth, and understanding.

This chapter explores the concept of reality, focusing on how our perceptions shape our personal realities and how we can shift our perspective to live more fulfilling and empowered lives. By changing the way we view ourselves and the world around us, we can transform the way we experience life.

Nestled between rolling green hills, there was a mystical village known as Vidyapur, famous for its serene lake—The Mirror of the Sky. Legends whispered that the lake reflected the truth of the world, revealing reality as it truly was.

People travelled from distant lands to gaze into its waters, hoping to find wisdom, clarity, or the answers to their deepest questions. The lake, however, did not offer simple answers.

Instead, it revealed a reflection unique to each person, shaped by their own beliefs, experiences, and emotions.

The Story: The Mirror of the Lake

One day, four travellers—each wise in their own way—arrived at the village, seeking the truth about reality. Hearing of the lake's legend, they sought out Devi, the village elder, a woman known for her deep wisdom and insight.

"Show us the truth of the world," they requested.

Devi, smiling gently, led them to the edge of the lake and said, "Look into the water and tell me what you see."

Each traveller knelt by the lake and peered into its still waters, expecting a singular truth. But what they saw was vastly different from one another.

The first traveller was Rajan, a wealthy merchant who had spent his life trading rare silks and jewels. As he gazed into the water, his reflection shimmered with golden hues. The ripples sparkled like silver coins, and the sunlight danced like flames of prosperity.

"The world is a place of opportunity," Rajan declared. "Fortune favours those who seek it. Those who are wise enough to trade well, work hard, and seize their chances will always find success."

He turned to Devi with confidence. "This is the truth of the world. Life is a game of wealth and abundance."

The second traveller, Kavi, was a poet whose heart belonged to art, music, and beauty. As he gazed into the lake, he saw endless colours swirling like a painted sky—soft pinks, deep purples, and golden streaks stretching beyond the horizon. The reflection shimmered like poetry written in light.

With wonder in his voice, Kavi said, "The world is a masterpiece. It is beauty, art, and endless inspiration. The only truth worth knowing is that life is meant to be experienced and expressed through creativity."

He looked at Devi and smiled. "This is the truth I see."

The third traveller, Veer, was a warrior who had seen many battles. His hands bore the scars of war, and his heart carried the weight of fallen comrades. When he peered into the lake, he saw dark storm clouds reflected in its waters. Waves crashed against the shore, and the wind howled like a war cry.

His face hardened. "The world is a battlefield," Veer said grimly. "Only the strong survive. Life is not about wealth or beauty—it is about power, struggle, and the ability to endure hardship."

He turned to Devi, his voice firm. "This is the only truth."

The fourth traveller, Anirudh, was a philosopher who had spent years in contemplation, seeking the nature of truth itself. He watched the others speak, then turned to the lake and gazed into its depths. At first, he saw shifting images—golden prosperity, artistic beauty, fierce storms. But as he looked deeper, the water stilled, and his own face stared back at him.

A realisation dawned upon him. He turned to Devi and said, "The world is but a reflection of the self. We see only a part of reality—our own reality."

Devi nodded, pleased with their answers. "You have all spoken your truth," she said. "But none of you has seen the whole picture."

She gestured towards the lake. "Reality is not one thing— it is many things at once. Each of you looked into the same water, yet saw something different. What you see in the world is shaped by your mind, your heart, and your experiences. The merchant sees wealth, the poet sees beauty, the warrior sees struggle, and the philosopher sees reflection. None of you is wrong, yet none of you see everything."

The four travellers fell silent, contemplating her words.

"To truly understand reality," Devi continued, "one must look beyond their own reflection. The world is vast, ever-changing, and filled with countless perspectives. If you only trust your own view, you will never see the full truth. But if you learn to see through the eyes of others, to embrace different perspectives, then—and only then—will you begin to understand the nature of reality."

The travellers bowed to Devi, their hearts filled with newfound wisdom.

That night, as they sat by the lake under the stars, they no longer argued about whose truth was the greatest. Instead, they listened to each other, eager to understand the world beyond their own reflection.

And so, the Mirror of the Sky continued to teach all who gazed into its waters—not by revealing one single truth, but by showing them the infinite ways in which reality could be seen.

Key Concepts: The Subjective Nature of Reality

Reality is a complex and multifaceted concept. Our personal experiences, beliefs, and emotions influence the way we perceive and interact with the world. It's important to recognise that each person's reality is shaped by their unique viewpoint, past experiences, and emotional state.

Let's explore four perspectives on reality that can help you shift your mindset and approach life in a more empowering way.

The Perspective of Beliefs

Our beliefs are the filter through which we interpret the world. These beliefs are often formed early in life based on our experiences, culture, and teachings. For example, if you believe that the world is a dangerous place, you will likely perceive even neutral situations as threatening. Believing in abundance makes you more likely to notice opportunities and possibilities.

Our beliefs are not truths but perceptions—created by us. They have the power to shape the reality we experience. If you hold limiting beliefs, such as "I am not good enough" or "I will never succeed," you may find it difficult to achieve your goals or build fulfilling relationships. On the other hand, if you cultivate empowering beliefs, such as "I am worthy of success" or "I am capable of growth," your reality shifts towards a more positive and abundant experience.

Challenge your beliefs. Question them and ask yourself: Are these beliefs serving me, or are they limiting me? By consciously changing the beliefs that no longer serve you, you can begin to see a different, more empowering reality.

The Perspective of Emotions

Our emotions colour our perception of reality. When we feel angry or fearful, our view of the world tends to be clouded by those emotions. We may perceive people or situations as hostile or threatening, even if they are not. Conversely, when we feel joyful or calm, we are more likely to see the world as a friendly and welcoming place.

Emotions are powerful forces shaping how we interpret events and interact with others. They often distort our sense of reality, creating a feedback loop where negative emotions perpetuate negative perceptions, and positive emotions lead to positive outcomes.

Learn to manage your emotions. Practice mindfulness and emotional awareness to recognise when your emotions influence your perception of reality. By stepping back and creating space between your emotional reactions and your responses, you can choose to see things more objectively and with a clearer perspective.

The Perspective of Experiences

Our past experiences shape the way we perceive new situations. For example, if you've had negative experiences in relationships, you may be more cautious and sceptical when entering new ones. If you've experienced failure, you may be more afraid to take risks in the future.

However, our experiences are not the final determinant of our reality. Just because something happened in the past doesn't mean it will happen again in the future. Our memories can be distorted, and the emotional charge attached to past events can cloud our ability to see things objectively.

Recognise that your past does not define your future. Instead of allowing past experiences to dictate how you see new opportunities, approach them with fresh eyes. Cultivate a mindset of curiosity and openness, knowing that every new experience is unique and separate from the past.

The Perspective of Context

The context in which we find ourselves plays a crucial role in shaping our perception of reality. Our environment, cultural norms, and societal influences create a framework through which we view the world. For instance, if you grow up in an environment where success is measured by material wealth, you might see people with wealth as more successful or important, regardless of their personal happiness or fulfilment.

Cultural norms also shape the way we perceive relationships, success, and happiness. For example, some cultures prioritise family above individual goals, while others encourage independence and personal achievement. These societal contexts influence our definition of success, happiness, and fulfilment.

Recognise that the cultural and societal contexts you live in can influence how you see yourself and others. Be aware of your internalised norms and expectations, and question whether they align with your values. Choose to define your own reality, based on your own truth rather than external pressures.

Key Understandings of the Concept of Reality

Reality Is Subjective – Reality is not a fixed or absolute truth; it is shaped by our perceptions, beliefs, emotions, experiences, and societal influences. Each individual's view of the world is unique.

Perception Shapes Experience – How we perceive events, people, and situations determines how we experience them. Shifting our perspective can shift our experience of reality.

Changing Your Reality Starts with Changing Your Lens – To change your reality, you must first change the lens through which you view the world. This can be done by shifting your beliefs, managing your emotions, letting go of past experiences, and questioning societal expectations.

Reality Is Not Set in Stone – Your current reality is not permanent. By shifting your mindset and changing your perspective, you can create a new reality that aligns with your goals, values, and desires.

The way we perceive reality has a profound impact on how we live. By shifting our perspectives, we can change our experiences, break free from limiting beliefs, and create a life filled with more clarity, possibility, and joy. Ultimately, reality is not something external to us but something we create with our thoughts, beliefs, and actions. When we become aware of this power, we can choose to see the world in a way that serves our growth and happiness.